Mathematical development

Seasonal activities

Thérèse Finlay and
Jacquie Finlay

Seasonal ideas ◆ Festival activities ◆ Early learning goals

CREDITS

British Library Cataloguing-in-Publication Data
A catalogue record for this book is available from the British Library.

ISBN 0 439 01899 4

AUTHORS
Thérèse Finlay and Jacquie Finlay

EDITOR
Clare Miller

ASSISTANT EDITOR
Saveria Mezzana

SERIES DESIGNER
Anna Oliwa

DESIGNER
Narinder Sandhu

ILLUSTRATIONS
Anna Hopkins

COVER ILLUSTRATION
Anna Hopkins

ACKNOWLEDGEMENTS
The publishers gratefully acknowledge permission to reproduce the following copyright material:

Jill Townsend for 'Conkers' by Jill Townsend from *Playtime Poems* edited by John Foster © 1995, Jill Townsend (1995, OUP)

Published by Scholastic Ltd, Villiers House, Clarendon Avenue, Leamington Spa, Warwickshire CV32 5PR

Designed using Adobe Pagemaker
Printed by Proost NV, Belgium

Visit our website at www.scholastic.co.uk

1 2 3 4 5 6 7 8 9 0   1 2 3 4 5 6 7 8 9 0

CONTENTS

Around the year

The aims of the series

This book forms part of a series of six books that provide practical activities to support the Early Learning Goals (QCA). Each of the six books focuses on a different area of learning. The ideas presented can be applied equally well to the documents on pre-school education published for Scotland, Wales and Northern Ireland. As the title suggests, the books are intended to be used throughout the year, with activities and ideas for each of the four seasons and the multicultural festivals and special days that fall within them.

The teaching of the seasons (and their associated activities) has long been established as an important part of learning. The ideas contained in this series of books provide new and interesting twists to the familiar themes of the seasons, as well as considering some of the most popular and less well-known multicultural festivals and feast days. Practitioners will find the activities an invaluable source of new ideas that can be dipped into at any time throughout the year.

Mathematics

The focus on mathematics around the year will stimulate the children's imagination through a selection of cross-curricular activities. Opportunities for early mathematical experiences will be provided through activities such as counting leaves fallen from trees in Autumn, sorting candles for a Divali celebration, matching animals to their young in spring, ordering snowmen in winter and using shapes to design a prayer mat for the celebration of Eid-ul-Fitr. A brief description of each festival covered and the date that they are celebrated has been provided on pages 7 and 8.

How to use this book

This book is divided into four main chapters – one for each of the seasons. For the purpose of the book the seasons are divided as follows:

- ◆ Chapter 1 – Spring (March, April and May)
- ◆ Chapter 2 – Summer (June, July and August)
- ◆ Chapter 3 – Autumn (September, October and November)

- ◆ Chapter 4 – Winter (December, January and February)

Each chapter provides 14 activities (one per page). Six of these activities are linked specifically to the season in question and the other eight activities are linked to festivals associated with

that time of year. Each activity page provides a comprehensive list of the resources that will be needed, as well as instructions outlining the preparation that would be required and a step-by-step guide of how to teach and manage the work. Where an activity involves cooking or handling of food, this symbol ! will remind you to check for any allergies and dietary requirements.

Supporting and extending learning

The activity ideas are aimed at four-year-olds with support and extension suggestions for three- and five-year-olds. The extension ideas may also include suggestions for follow-up activities to continue, extend or reinforce the children's learning. Many of the activities may be adapted to suit any age group, with more or less adult intervention required for the children to experience success.

Using the photocopiable activities

The 16 photocopiable pages provide a range of resources to support the activities. They cover a variety of different learning opportunities. There is a poem ('Conkers', on page 74), linked to Autumn, and while some of the photocopiables are intended to be used as games (such as 'Budding flowers', on page 68), others are suitable for discovering and recording information (such as 'Fill us up!', on page 80). Guidelines on how many copies of each sheet you need are included in the 'What you need' or 'Preparation' sections.

Links with home

For each activity there are suggestions for 'home links'. These are ways of linking the work to the children's home environment and including their parents and carers in the work that is undertaken in the setting.

This partnership with parents and carers is an important way to provide continuity with the children's home lives and their time with you. The children will benefit greatly from having their learning reinforced within the home.

There are also suggestions as to how to enlist the help of parents and carers for many of the activities performed regularly in your group setting.

Festivals

St Patrick's Day (17 March)
An Irish celebration of their patron saint who rid Ireland of all snakes. Shamrock is worn (St Patrick used it to explain the Christian belief in the Holy Trinity).

Purim (March)
Jewish festival commemorating how the Jewish people were saved from death by Queen Esther. Music, plays and carnivals are part of the celebrations and Hamantashen (cakes filled with poppy seeds) are made and eaten.

Mother's Day (March/April)
Once a holiday for servant girls to visit their mothers with gifts, it is now a time to show love and appreciation to mothers or female carers by making cards and giving presents.

Holi (March/April)
Holi is a Hindu festival that lasts one to five days and remembers Prahlada who refused to worship the king regardless of the punishment. Holi traditions today include throwing paint and coloured water over each other.

Easter (March/April)
The most important Christian festival when Jesus' return to life is celebrated. People give chocolate eggs as a symbol of new life.

Baisakhi (14 April)
The Sikh New Year festival commemorating the five volunteers that offered to sacrifice themselves at Guru Gobind Singh's request. Also marks the introduction of the Khalsa.

Hanamatsuri (April)
A Japanese flower festival celebrating the birth of Buddha. Baby Buddha images are placed in floral shrines symbolizing the garden in which the Buddha was born.

Kodomono-hi/Japanese Children's Day (5 May)
A Japanese festival to celebrate the health and strength of the children. Carp-shaped kites are flown from poles in gardens, one for each son.

Wesak (May/June)
Theravada Buddhists celebrate the birth, enlightenment and death of the Buddha on this day. People decorate their temples and homes with candles, flowers and incense.

Shavuot (May/June)
A Jewish festival celebrating the revelation of the Ten Commandments to Moses on Mount Sinai. Synagogues are decorated with dairy foods, fruit and flowers.

Midsummer's Day (24 June)
Falls shortly after the longest day of the year. Druids still meet at Stonehenge for sunrise. Traditions include bonfires, feasts and torchlit processions.

Father's Day (June)
Children give love and thanks to their fathers during this modern festival.

Dragon Boat Festival (June)
A Chinese festival honouring Ch'u Yuan who drowned himself in protest at the Emperor. Today dragon boat races symbolize the rush to save him.

O-bon (July/August)
A Japanese Buddhist festival when the spirits of the ancestors are welcomed home on an annual visit. Celebrations include lighting lanterns and bonfires.

Raksha Bandhan (July/August)
A Hindu festival when girls tie a rakhi (bracelet) around their brothers' wrists to protect them and the brothers promise to protect their sisters.

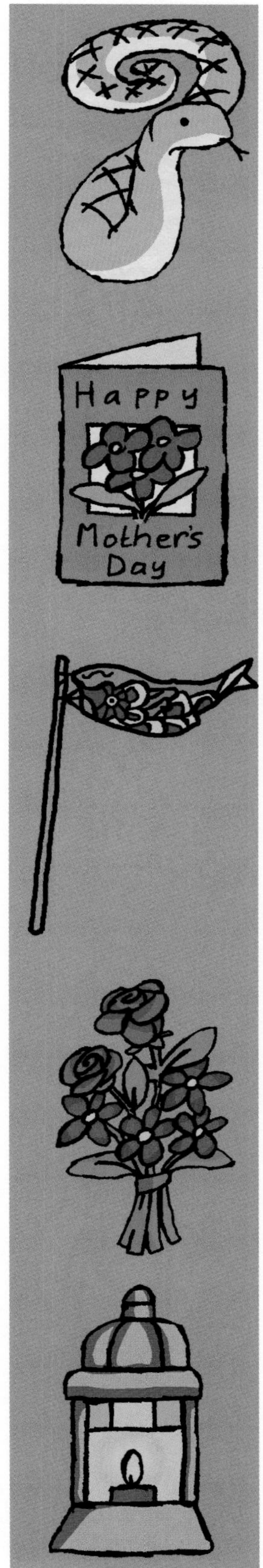

Janamashtami (July/August/September)
A Hindu festival when Krishna's birth is commemorated. A statue or picture of the infant Krishna is placed in a cradle and everyone files past to rock the cradle.

Grandparent's Day (September)
This is a modern festival in which children and families thank their grandparents by making cards and sending them gifts.

Yom Kippur (September)
This is the final day of the ten days of repentance and the holiest day in the Jewish calendar, when Jews ask God to forgive their sins. After a special family meal, people go to the synagogue to pray.

Sukkot (September/October)
A Jewish festival that commemorates the people's journey in the wilderness after escaping from Egypt. Temporary shelters are built and harvest is celebrated.

Harvest Festival (September/October)
A time of thanksgiving for the harvesting of crops. Traditions include harvest suppers and giving of food to the needy.

Navaratri (September/October)
Navaratri means 'nine nights', which is how long this Hindu festival lasts. It commemorates the victory of Rama over the demon king Ravana.

Divali (October/November)
Hindus remember the story of Rama and Sita. Sikhs celebrate the sixth Guru, Guru Hargobind's escape from imprisonment. Homes are decorated with divas (lamps).

Bonfire Night (5 November)
A British celebration, sometimes called 'Guy Fawkes Night', which remembers a historical event when a group of men led by Guy Fawkes attempted to blow up the Houses of Parliament in 1605.

Hanukkah (November/December)
Jewish festival of light lasting eight days, commemorating the reclamation of the temple from the Syrians and the miracle of the temple light that burned for eight days on a small amount of oil.

Christmas Day (25 December)
Christian festival celebrating the birth of Jesus. People decorate their homes and exchange gifts as a reminder of those given to Jesus.

Eid-ul-Fitr (December/January)
Muslim festival held at the end of Ramadan. People wear new clothes, visit family and friends, exchange gifts and cards and eat a celebratory meal.

New Year (1 January)
New Year is celebrated with parties and the traditional singing of 'Auld Lang Syne'. People reflect on the past and make resolutions for the future.

Epiphany (6 January)
Celebrates the revelation to the Gentiles of Jesus Christ as the Saviour, as portrayed by the coming of the Three Wise Men. It is the Twelfth Day, traditionally the end of the Christmas season, when all decorations are taken down.

Chinese New Year (January/February)
The most important Chinese festival, lasting 15 days. Families clean and decorate their homes, wear new clothes and visit family and friends.

Valentine's Day (14 February)
The patron saint of lovers' day is celebrated by sending anonymous cards and gifts to loved ones. Valentine was probably a roman soldier that refused to agree not to marry.

Shrove Tuesday (February/March)
Falls on the day before the Christian period of Lent. People use up certain foods to make pancakes. Celebrations include an elaborate carnival.

Hop, hop and away

What you need

The song 'Five Little Speckled Frogs' (traditional); play dough; boards; aprons; protective table covering; number cards; selection of different-shaped plastic lids or shaped card; pictures of tadpoles.

Preparation

Cover a table with protective cloth. Lay out the boards and place a ball of play dough on each.

What to do

Sing 'Five Little Speckled Frogs' with the children and explain that frogs develop from tadpoles. Show them pictures of tadpoles, and tell them that they are going to make five little tadpoles of their own. Ask the children to each sit in front of a board and ball of play dough. Show them how to roll a small piece of dough into a sausage shape, flattening the end with their fingers. Challenge the children to choose a 'pond' (plastic lid or shaped card) and make five tadpoles to go in it. Encourage the children to describe or name the shape using language such as 'It is round', 'It is square' and 'It is nearly round'.

Once the task is complete discuss with the children the different-shaped ponds and ask them to guess which one holds the most tadpoles. After some discussion and counting, the children should realize that although the ponds look different, there are still five tadpoles in each one. During this activity, it is important to provide opportunities for the children to explain their predictions and reasoning, for example: 'The square pond is big but the circle is small, so it looks like there are more tadpoles in the circle'.

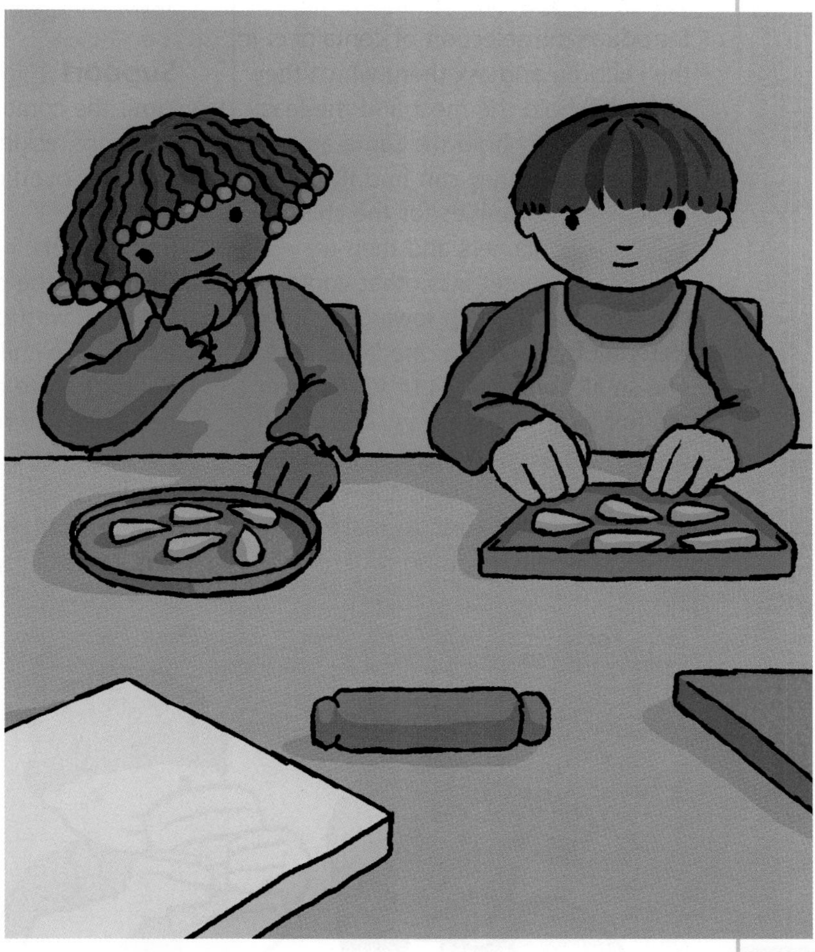

Support

Roll sausages of play dough, ready for the children to flatten to make tadpoles.

Extension

Show the children number cards up to 5 and ask them to add the corresponding number of tadpoles to their ponds.

Learning objective
To separate a group of objects in different ways, beginning to recognize that the total is still the same.

Group size
Small groups

Home links
Ask parents and carers to visit local ponds with their child to see if they can spot any tadpoles or frogs. Invite the children to bring in pictures or books about frogs and tadpoles.

Buckets full

Learning objective
To order two items by capacity.

Group size
Small groups of no more than four children.

What you need

Water trough; food colouring; range of containers and plastic bottles; aprons; mop; bucket; pebbles and marbles.

Preparation

Colour water using food colouring and pour into a water trough. Place containers around the edge, within easy access for the children.

What to do

Introduce the selection of containers to the children and ask them which they think will hold the most and the least water. Will any hold the same amount? Ask them how they can find this out. Provide opportunities for the children to fill the containers and then try pouring the water into other containers.

Direct the children towards making a waterfall by choosing one large and one small container. Pour water from the full large container into the small container placed in the water trough until it overflows to create a waterfall. Challenge the children to make different waterfalls using different containers. Can they make ones that last longer or are higher?

Explain to the children that waterfalls can also be made by half-filling a container with water and then adding pebbles or marbles until the water flows over the top. Provide time for the children to investigate how much water and pebbles are needed to make the best waterfall. Remember to take care when using pebbles or marbles with small children.

Support

Limit the container choice to teapots and cups, asking the children to make the cups overflow.

Extension

Challenge the children to make a tall waterfall with different layers. This will require the children to think carefully about the size of the containers and how they will need to arrange and balance them. Ensure that you offer guidance and suggestions to the children who need them to complete this successfully.

Home links
Inform parents and carers of the work the group has undertaken and ask them to help their children to make waterfalls during bathtime or when washing up.

Rain or shine?

What you need

Selection of weather rhymes, poems and songs, such as *An Orange Poetry Paintbox* chosen by John Foster (Oxford University Press); large sheet of card; drawing and colouring materials; paper or whiteboard; Velcro; collage materials; glue; scissors; aprons; protective table covering; photocopiable sheet on page 65.

Preparation

Make a large chart by writing the days of the week on the landscape sheet of card and attaching a piece of Velcro below each day (to display the weather symbols later on). Make enough copies of the photocopiable sheet so that you have one for each child.

What to do

Sing and say a selection of weather rhymes with the children, such as 'Rain, Rain Go Away', 'Incy Wincy Spider', 'The Sun Has Got His Hat On', 'Here We Go Round the Mulberry Bush' and so on.

Ask the children to think about the different types of weather they have seen and talk about what they like about different types of days, for example, playing in the sun, flying kites on windy days, splashing in the rain and so on. Record these onto paper or a whiteboard and discuss the symbols that could be used for each one.

Let the children work individually or in small groups to use a range of collage materials to decorate the weather-symbol templates on page 65. For example, they could use cotton wool for the cloud, shiny gold foil for the sun, Cellophane or silver foil for the rain and small leaf cut-outs and brown corrugated card for the tree in the wind. When the weather symbols are dry, cut them out, stick a piece of Velcro onto the back of each one and attach them to the chart.

Each day look at the weather with the children and together decide what it is like and which weather symbol would best represent it. Ask a different child each day to choose a version of the correct weather symbol to attach to the chart. Towards the end of the week, the children can begin to make comparisons between the type of weather seen so far and make predictions based on this knowledge.

Support

Offer help to the children when collaging materials.

Extension

Ask a group of children to predict the weather for the next three days and then compare this forecast at the end of the week with the actual weather.

Learning objective
To record information and use it to make comparisons and predictions.

Group size
Large or small groups.

Home links
Ask parents and carers to watch the weather forecast on television with their child or point it out in a newspaper. Invite parents and carers to attend a 'weather assembly' where the children sing weather songs and perhaps perform simple dances.

Whose house?

Learning objectives
To develop mathematical language; to choose suitable components to make a particular model.

Group size
Small groups.

What you need

Selection of construction kits, both large and small; pictures of animals and their young; card; drawing and writing materials; small-world play animals.

Preparation

Mount animal pictures and place them next to the appropriate construction kit.

What to do

Discuss with the children types of animals that are born during springtime, such as chicks and lambs. Look at the selection of pictures and encourage the children to suggest where the animals and their young would live.

Looking at the pictures as a guide, consider with the children the size of the different animals and what size and shape their house would need to be for them to fit comfortably. For example, chicks would need a small round house, worms would need a long thin house, rabbits would need a tall house to accommodate their ears, and so on.

Using a construction kit, show the children how to build an animal house. Make this easily recognizable so that the children can guess which animal would live in the house.

Now provide plenty of time for the children to build homes for spring animals of their choice. They should then write or draw labels on the card saying who lives there. Ask the children to display these cards by the entrances to their houses.

To develop the idea further, mix up the children's labels and challenge them to rearrange them next to the correct houses.

Support

Use large construction kits, which the children have had a chance to become familiar with.

Extension

Encourage the children to use a range of mathematical language to describe the shape and position of the different houses when they are displayed.

Home links
Arrange a visit to a local farm to look closely at the animal homes there and invite parents and carers to accompany their children on the day out.

Sand flowers

What you need
Sand tray; selection of resources for making and pressing into the sand, such as lollipop sticks, feathers, pebbles, coins, shells, straws, pencils, wooden blocks and so on.

Preparation
Dampen the sand with water, flatten and smooth the surface. Carefully arrange the objects so that they are close to the tray and clearly visible to the children.

What to do
Say the rhyme 'Mary, Mary, Quite Contrary' with the children and ask them what types of flowers grow in their gardens if they have them or in local parks. If they are unsure of the names of the flowers, invite them to describe the shapes, sizes and colours of the petals and leaves.

Explain to the children that they are going to make some flower patterns in the sand using objects from the range on display. Encourage them to think carefully about the different shapes and sizes they could create. After each child has been given the chance to create a flower, demonstrate how to make a flower that incorporates a repeating pattern such as: a pebble centre, straw, feather, straw, feather and so on for the petals, and coins for the stem. Allow the children time to make their own flower patterns in the sand.

Once the children are familiar with making flowers, they can use the materials to experiment with printing repeating patterns in the sand.

Support
Limit the amount of resources available to two or three objects and encourage the children to make very simple patterns.

Extension
Encourage the children to work in pairs, with one child starting a pattern for the other to complete.

Learning objectives
To begin to use mathematical names and terms to describe 2D shapes; to talk about, recognize and re-create simple patterns.

Group size
Small groups of no more than four children.

Home links
Ask the children to bring in flowers from their gardens at home to study the shapes, colours and patterns. Ask the parents and carers to send in any flowered wrapping paper or wallpaper which could be used for cutting and sticking activities or to make simple matching games.

Jumping Jacks

Learning objectives
To introduce the measurement of time; to use developing mathematical ideas and methods to solve practical problems.

Group size
Any size.

What you need
Three different-sized funnels; dry sand; a selection of containers; large sheet of card; writing materials; a large open space.

Preparation
Check that the dry sand runs freely through the funnels and collects in a container below. Draw three different-sized funnels onto the large sheet of card so that you can record the children's names later on.

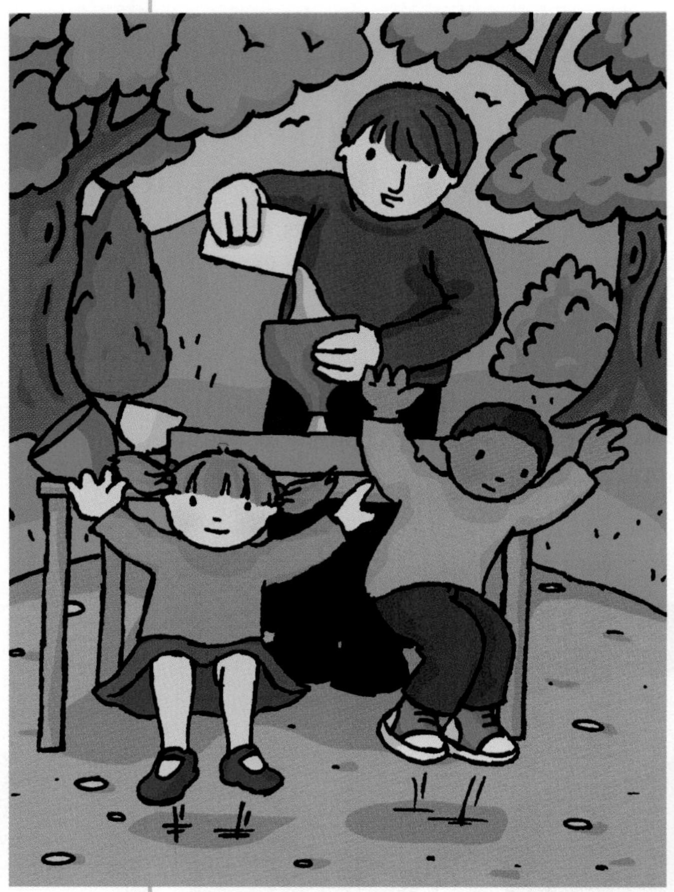

What to do
On a fine spring morning, take the children outside into a large open space and let them observe the sky, trees, birds and so on. Encourage them to take deep breaths as they discuss how spring weather makes them feel. Talk about the spring breathing new life into nature and suggest that such a morning might fill people as well as the animals with energy!

Show the children how to jump with their feet together. Allow time for them to practise jumping around the space and on the spot. Gather together a small group of children and set them off jumping. Explain that you want to see who can keep jumping for the longest time!

When all the children have stopped jumping, introduce the sand and the funnels, telling the children that you are going to pour the sand through the small funnel and they must try to keep jumping while the sand runs through. Repeat the activity but this time using the next-sized funnel. Repeat this process again for the last funnel.

To assess the children's understanding, ask questions such as, 'Why does the longest funnel take a long time for the sand to run through?', 'Which funnel takes the longest time for the sand to run through?', 'Who is able to jump for the longest time?', 'Which funnel makes you feel most tired?', 'How else could you move as the sand runs through the funnel?' and so on.

Finally, encourage the children to tell you how long they can jump, for example, 'I can jump as long as the biggest funnel', 'I can hop as long as the smallest funnel' and so on, and write the children's names on the appropriate funnel on the piece of card.

Support
It may be necessary to hold the children's hands and jump with them.

Extension
Encourage the children to count how many jumps they can do in the given period of time.

Home links
Ask parents and carers to encourage their child to practise jumping, hopping and skipping and to count how many jumps they can do.

Slithering snake sort

Learning objective
To use mathematical ideas and methods to solve practical problems

Group size
Small groups.

What you need

Card; paint; paintbrushes; aprons; protective table covering; pictures of snakes; scissors; plastic printing shapes; writing materials.

Preparation

Show the children pictures of different snakes, encouraging them to use descriptive language to describe each picture. Ensure that the table is covered and the children are wearing aprons.

What to do

Tell the children the legend of how St Patrick cleared Ireland of snakes by leading them to a high cliff so that they would fall into the sea.

Provide the children with a sheet of card each and ask them to paint or print a large colourful snake. Encourage them to make all the snakes different, suggesting a range of different types including long, thin, fat, short, coloured, striped, spotty, square, patterned and so on. When all the snake paintings are dry, cut them out to be used for a sorting activity.

Lay the snakes out so they can be clearly seen. Ask the children which snakes are similar and could therefore be grouped together. Now sort the snakes for the children according to one criterion, such as long. Ask the children to guess how you have sorted the snakes. Once the children are confident at doing this, sort the snakes by two or more different criteria for the children to identify.

Allow the children to try sorting the snakes according to their own criteria. Invite them to work in pairs, each child in turn sorting the snakes for their partner to guess.

Support

Limit both the colour and type of snake used. In some instances, it may be appropriate to provide templates for the children to use when drawing their snakes.

Extension

Challenge the children to sort the snakes themselves using two or more criteria, for example, long and fat.

Home links
Ask parents and carers to try sorting with the children at home using toys, household objects and small-world play equipment. This could be incorporated into tidying-up times. Ask parents and carers to look in the cupboards at home with their children to see how things are sorted, for example, one cupboard of pans, one of food, one of dishes, a drawer of cutlery and so on.

Throw and count

Learning objective
In practical activities and discussion begin to use the vocabulary involved in adding and subtracting

Group size
Small groups in pairs.

What you need
Selection of dice – large, small, coloured, spotted or numbered; photocopiable sheet on page 66; card; colouring and writing materials.

Preparation
Make one copy for each child of the photocopiable sheet. Label the parts of Queen Esther with numbers appropriate for the age and ability of the children. Ensure that there are enough spotted dice to give one to each child. (It may be necessary to make dice spotted 1–3, using wooden cubes and either sticky labels or felt-tipped pens).

What to do
Introduce the selection of dice to the children. Pass them around and encourage the children to look at them closely, talking about what they are used for and how they are different from one another. Explain to the children that they are going to use some of the dice to make a nice, colourful Queen Esther.

Provide each child with a photocopiable sheet, colouring materials and a dice. Sort the children into pairs of similar mathematical ability. Point out the different numbered parts of the face, crown and hair and explain that the pairs of children must throw both their dice, add the numbers together, and colour the part of the picture that corresponds to that number.

Support
Adapt Queen Esther by labelling sections with spots instead of numerals. In addition, or alternatively, invite the children to play the game using just one dice.

Extension
Extend the activity by using higher numbers and one spotted and one numbered dice. Once the children have completed a round by adding the numbers together, they could try finding a total by taking the smaller number from the larger one.

Home links
Ask parents and carers to lend dice games to your setting for the children to play with each other.

How many pieces?

Learning objective
To use mathematical language to describe the shape and size of flat shapes.

Group size
Any size.

What you need

Swiss roll; selection of sweets for decoration; knife; chopping board; fondant icing; food colouring; icing sugar; rolling pin; cake board; aprons; protective table covering.

Preparation

Cover the table with the protective cloth, wash the children's hands and put on aprons. Colour the fondant icing by adding food colouring and kneading.

What to do

Explain to the children that they are going to make a 'flower cake', to take home for their mums to celebrate Mother's Day. Briefly explain that this is a special day when we think about our mothers or special people that take care of us. This may be a sensitive issue for some children and so special care should be taken.

Show the children how to make the petals of the cake by cutting pieces of a Swiss roll and placing these next to each other to form a flower shape. While you are cutting the cake, encourage the children to discuss how many petals are needed if each child is to have one and where they should be placed. Then, invite them to talk about all the important things about their mum or special person.

Once the flower is arranged on the cake board, roll out the coloured fondant icing to cover each petal and ask each child to decorate a petal with sweets. During this activity, reference could be made to the size and shape of the petals and cake, how the Swiss roll could be shared out between more children and how a petal could be shared between two and then four children. Invite each child to take a petal home as a gift for their mum or special person.

Support

Use fairy cakes instead and give one to each child to decorate as they wish.

Extension

Encourage the children to roll out their own icing, or spread buttercream on each petal. They could also share a given number of sweets between the available petals.

Home links
Make a gift bag to send the cake home to mums. Help the children to make an invitation for their mums to attend a special Mother's Day celebration.

Colour explosion

Learning objective
To recognize colours and experience colour mixing.

Group size
Small groups.

What you need
Powder paint in a selection of colours; paper; water; sponges; paintbrushes; spoons; aprons; protective table covering.

Preparation
Cover your working area with protective table covering and make sure all the children are wearing aprons.

What to do
Explain to the children that the custom during Holi is for people to run through the villages, banging on doors and windows and throwing coloured water and paint at their friends and neighbours. Tell the children that we can't throw paint at each other and so we are going to 'throw' it at the paper instead. Provide them with paper and wet sponges, telling them to dampen the paper with the sponge. Invite them to sprinkle coloured powder paint onto the wet paper using spoons or paintbrushes and to watch what happens. Notice how the colour spreads and how it looks like it is exploding.

Let the children experiment with two primary colours and ask them if they think that these, together, will make a new colour. What might this colour be? Will it be light or dark? Does it make a difference which colour we sprinkle first? How much powder paint do you need to use? Continue this activity, experimenting with different colours.

Support
Use a plant spray to dampen the paper and apply the powder paint with a brush, ensuring that the name of the colour is reinforced each time it is used or created through mixing.

Extension
Challenge the children to create a repeating colour pattern by alternating colours and letting them mix as part of the pattern, so they might have blue, green, yellow, blue, green, yellow and so on.

Home links
Provide coloured Cellophane for parents and carers to use at home to make colour binoculars with their children, by attaching it to the end of two kitchen roll tubes that are secured together.

We're going on an egg hunt!

What you need

Selection of small baskets; card; writing materials; chocolate or sugared eggs; a toy chicken.

Preparation

Hide the eggs so that they are not too easy to find and ask the children to wash their hands.

What to do

Sing the song 'Chick, Chick, Chick, Chick, Chicken, Lay a Little Egg for Me' with the children and tell them that the chicken has laid eggs for them and they have to go on an egg hunt in order to find them. Show the children the baskets and ask them how many eggs they think each one will hold. Ask them if they think that the chicken will have laid enough eggs. Will the eggs be big or little? Will the size of the eggs make a difference to how many will fit in the basket?

Challenge a small group of children to choose a basket and begin hunting. While the children are searching, encourage them to think about where the chicken may have laid the eggs, using positional language in their discussion. Talk about whether the eggs might be under chairs, in a cupboard, behind a table, on top of some shelves and so on, directing their attention to those places as they are mentioned.

When the children have filled the basket, encourage them to guess how many eggs are in it, then invite them to count them to see if their estimation was close.

Support

Hide only large eggs wrapped in yellow tissue paper so that the children can find them more easily.

Extension

Encourage the children to record their estimation by drawing eggs in a basket. When they have collected the eggs, ask them to match these drawings to the eggs in their basket.

Learning objectives
To use everyday words to describe position; to show confidence and offer solutions to problems.

Group size
Any size.

Home links
Invite the children to enter a competition for the best decorated hard-boiled egg.

Encourage parents and carers to use positional language at home with their children.

Ask the children to find out from home how many ways an egg can be cooked. This could be recorded through pictures.

Colourful soldiers

Learning objective
To use mathematical ideas and methods to solve practical problems and make comparisons.

Group size
Small groups.

What you need
Card; photocopiable sheet page 67; scissors; colouring materials; pair of plain shorts; comb; bracelet; turban made from a piece of material; sword made from cardboard and silver foil.

Preparation
Make four copies of the photocopiable sheet and colour them so that you have 16 different soldiers: colour all the soldiers' bodies on one sheet red with a different colour – red, blue, green and yellow – for each turban; colour all the soldiers' bodies on the next sheet blue, again with a different colour for each turban, and so on. Cut them out.

What to do
Introduce the different items worn by Sikh soldiers. Explain that each item has a different significance:

- Uncut hair and beard – to show that they love God;
- A comb – to demonstrate cleanliness;
- A steel bracelet – to show their strength;
- Sword – to remind them to protect the weak;
- Shorts – to move around easily.

Provide each child with a soldier card to discuss, paying close attention to what he is wearing.

Challenge the children to group the soldiers and, as the task is performed, focus on particular attributes. Once the children are familiar with the soldier cards, place one on the floor and ask the children to find a soldier to stand next to the first that has one difference from it. This should be repeated until all the cards are used or until there are none that can follow in sequence.

Think about the five items that Sikhs must wear as part of their uniform. Ask the children to count how many items of clothing they are wearing that day.

Support
Make simple groupings of soldiers, matching either body or turban colours.

Extension
Provide the children with copies of the photocopiable sheet and ask them to colour the soldiers themselves, ensuring that each has a different combination of colours.

Home links
Ask the children to find out if any family members wears a uniform for work, and if so, why – for protection, so that they can be identified, and so on. Perhaps the children could borrow the uniform, or part of it, to show and discuss with the other children at your setting.

Budding flowers

Learning objective
To count up to five objects by saying one number name for each item.

Group size
Four children.

What you need

Photocopiable sheet page 68; coloured paper in four different colours; scissors.

Preparation

Make four copies of the photocopiable sheet, each on different-coloured paper. Cut out five discs from each colour of paper.

What to do

Provide each child with a Buddha sheet and ask them to name the colour of their sheet and count how many flowers are on it. Show them the cut-out discs and tell them that they are going to play a game covering each of their flowers with a disc that matches the colour of their sheet. Encourage the children to count how many discs they will need to do this.

Place all the coloured discs, mixed up, so that the children can reach them, and encourage them to take it in turns to close their eyes and choose a disc. If it is the same colour as their sheet, they can use it to cover one of their flowers; if not, they must put it back with the other discs. The winner is the first person to cover all their flowers. During this task, ask questions such as, 'How many flowers have you covered?', 'How many more do you need to cover in order to complete your sheet?', 'Who has the most flowers still showing?', 'Who has the fewest?' and so on.

Support

Play in pairs with only two colours of sheet and disc.

Extension

Extend the activity by numbering each set of coloured discs and each flower from 1 to 5 and asking the children to throw a dice to determine which of their flowers they should pick up.

Home links
Ask the children to bring flowers from home to make their own special flower garden. Ask parents and carers to plant flowers with their child at home.

Kodomono-hi/ Japanese Children's Day

Learning objective
To talk about, recognize and re-create simple patterns.

Group size
Small groups.

Fishing fun

What you need

Card; glue; aprons; protective table covering; scissors; small garden canes; sticky tape; selection of collage materials including feathers, coloured paper, shiny paper, cotton wool, straws, and so on; selection of writing and drawing materials.

Preparation

Cover the table and ensure that all the children are wearing their aprons. Place the collage materials in small tubs or baskets on the table to provide easy access for the children.

What to do

It is important that the children have some understanding of what a repeating pattern is. Make some simple patterns for the children to copy, using a selection of collage materials. Ask the children to describe each material, using all their senses. Encourage them to copy your simple pattern using the same materials. As they work, ask them to suggest examples of repeating patterns that they have come across, such as those on wallpaper, on clothes, roofs, floors and so on.

Invite the children to draw an oval shape onto their sheet of card and add a triangular tail, to make a fish. Tell the children it is now their turn to create a repeating pattern, by choosing two materials with which to decorate the fish. Throughout the activity, discuss the size, shape and colour of the fishes. When the fishes are complete, attach them to small garden canes and let the children take them outside to wave in the breeze.

Support

Help the children to fill the fish with random patterns of their choice, instead of repeating patterns, using all the collage materials.

Extension

Once the children gain confidence in creating repeating patterns, extend the activity by inviting them to use three or more of the collage materials.

Home links
Ask parents and carers to point out repeating patterns on supermarket shelves, pavements and so on when they are out with their children.

Chocolate, strawberry, vanilla

What you need
Card; brown sugar paper; selection of coloured crêpe and tissue paper; brown corrugated cardboard; paint; sponges; drawing and colouring materials; toy cash register; plastic or real coins; sticky tape or stapler; containers.

Preparation
Make a selection of '2D ice-creams' by drawing, colouring or sponge printing the ice-cream shape and laminating. Prepare a number of brown cones made from sugar paper. Use a selection of coloured crêpe and tissue paper to scrunch up balls for the ice-cream. Make wafers or chocolate flakes from corrugated cardboard. Label containers ready for the children to sort ice-creams. Make large examples of coins from card and laminate.

What to do
Explain to the children that as it is summer, the role-play area is going to become an ice-cream shop. Show them the cones, asking how much they think they should charge for the different types of ice-cream. Ask questions such as, 'Would a small ice-cream be more expensive than a large one?', 'How much would two flavours together cost?', 'If you add a flake is it more expensive?', 'Are all the flavours going to be the same price?', 'Are the ready-made 2D cones the same price as the others?' and so on.

When prices have been decided upon, introduce the large coins to the children. Explain how much each coin is worth and how many you would need to buy the different ice-creams. Now leave the children to role-play activities such as counting how many ice-creams of each flavour they have, sorting ice-cream colours, sharing ice-creams out, writing price lists and bills, making ice-creams, receiving money and giving change.

Support
For younger children, limit the coins used to large card one and two pences.

Extension
Extend the activity by making task cards for the children to follow, with instructions on how many ice-creams the children should buy, and which flavours. They must then work out what coins they will need and whether they should receive change.

Learning objective
To use the vocabulary of addition and subtraction in practical activities.

Group size
Small groups.

Home links
Ask parents and carers to involve their children in making shopping lists and carrying out the shopping, perhaps letting their children pay and receive change.

Catch a fish

Learning objective
To enjoy joining in with number rhymes and songs.

Group size
Small groups of no more than four children.

What you need

Water tray; small fishing nets; selection of plastic or wooden fish; blue food colouring; foam numbers; large sheets of card and writing materials; aprons; large copy of '1, 2, 3, 4, 5, Once I Caught a Fish Alive' (traditional).

Preparation

Dye water with blue food colouring and fill a water tray with it. Place the fish and foam numbers into the tray. Make large number cards numbered 1 to 5 and laminate them. Place them on a surface next to the water tray.

What to do

Introduce the traditional rhyme to the children and ask them to recite it with you. Repeat the numbers 1 to 5 with them. Hold up the large pre-prepared number cards and ask the children to name the numbers if they can.

Practise this to familiarize the group with the numerals. Encourage the children to begin counting from a different number each time. Use the large number cards to place numbers in order, then invite the children to place the correct number of plastic or wooden fish on each of the cards.

Now explain to the children that they are going take it in turns to catch a fish and then a foam number in sequence, using the fishing nets. As each number and each fish are caught, encourage the children to place them on the corresponding number card.

Ask questions such as, 'How many fish have been caught?', 'How many more are in the water?', 'Are there more fish in the water than have been caught?', 'How many more fish will be needed to make five?', 'What number comes after 3?', 'What number comes before 2?' and so on.

Support

Provide assistance for children who have difficulty using the net and let them practise carrying out this task separately before playing the game as part of a group. Instead of being asked to catch numerals, the children could just catch specified numbers of fish up to three.

Extension

Use numbers up to 10 rather than 5 with older children. If there are enough fish available, encourage the children to collect the corresponding number of fish to the foam number caught.

Home links
Ask parents to sing this and other counting rhymes at home, such as 'Five Currant Buns', 'Five Little Speckled Frogs' and 'One, Two, Buckle My Shoe'.

Pattern match

What you need

Selection of empty washing-up liquid bottles or plant sprays; containers of water such as water tray, jugs and funnel; access to paved areas; a copy of the photocopiable sheet on page 69 for each child; card; writing materials.

Preparation

Choose a sunny day to carry out this activity. Ensure all containers are washed thoroughly, and fill the water tray.

What to do

Explain to the children that as it is a hot sunny day, they are going to make patterns outside. Tell the children that they will have to make many different patterns as the sun will quickly make the patterns disappear.

Once outside, demonstrate how to fill the washing-up bottle with water using the funnel and the jug. Make patterns on the floor and walls to show the differences between straight, curved and zigzag lines, explaining that these could form part of their patterns. Allow time for the children to experiment with making their own patterns and becoming familiar with directing the water to where they want it to go.

Once the children are confident with this, ask them to make a specific pattern in a given place. Challenge them to work in pairs copying each other's patterns. Encourage them to think about the size, shape and length of their patterns. Ask questions such as, 'Was the pattern difficult or easy to make?', 'Is the pattern rounded or straight?' and so on.

Provide each child with a copy of the pattern card and ask them to reproduce one of the styles of line on the wall or floor. When the children have finished, challenge them to match each other's patterns to the lines on the card. Discuss whether the patterns were easy to recognize.

Support

Allow younger children to play freely with ready-filled washing-up bottles, to support their motor control and recognize the action used to make different patterns.

Extension

Encourage older children to create their own repeating pattern that includes different elements, such as straight, curved, straight, curved.

Learning objective
To talk about, recognize and re-create simple patterns

Group size
Any size.

Home links
Ask parents and carers to help their children notice patterns in their home environment, such as the curved lines on the inside of an onion, patterns on furnishings and packaging, and so on.

Sloshing numbers

Learning objective
To recognize and write numbers to 10.

Group size
Any size.

What you need

Large number cards; large and small paintbrushes; buckets and containers; paper; writing materials; large paved area outside.

Preparation

Ideally, carry out this activity on a sunny day. Fill the containers and buckets with water, place the paintbrushes close to the containers and position these around the space.

What to do

Invite the children to count forwards and backwards to 10 together. Look at each number card and encourage the children to try drawing the numeral in the air and on the palms of their hands with a finger. Encourage them to take turns choosing a number card, saying the number and then tracing it with their finger.

When the children are familiar with the way each number is formed, encourage them to practise forming each digit on the wall or floor with a paintbrush and water. As they are writing their numbers, inspire discussion with questions such as, 'What number are you writing?', 'Where does it begin?', 'Is it a high number or low number?', 'Is it more or less than four?', 'What number comes after it?', 'What number comes before it?' and so on.

Now tell the children to change the size of their brushes and paint the numbers 1 to 10 in sequence on the floor or wall. Add an extra challenge to see if they can finish the sequence before the sun dries up number 1!

Encourage the children to stop from time to time, to count the numbers they have formed so far in their number line.

Support

Draw an outline of the numbers with chalk for the children to trace over with their water and brushes.

Extension

Using chalk, draw part of a number line on the ground or wall. Provide water and brushes for the children and ask them to fill in the missing numbers in the line. Can they go any higher than the number 10?

Home links
Invite parents and carers to help their child practise writing numbers at home using a range of different media such as paint, crayons, felt-tipped pens, pencils, pasta, dried beans and so on.

Buzzzzzzzzz!

What you need
Card; paint; paintbrushes; tissue paper; PVA glue; sticky tape; writing and drawing materials; bubble wrap; blue backing paper; Velcro; aprons; selection of found materials for printing; paper; protective table covering.

Preparation
Attach backing paper to a suitable wall area. Cover a work surface with protective cloth and ensure all the children are wearing aprons.

What to do
Discuss with the children what insects and flies they see more of in the summer, and encourage them to think about why this might be the case.

Explain to the children that they are going to create a display around one type of insect – bees. Tell the group that bees like to gather pollen from flowers to make honey, and that this is why we only see them in spring and summer.

Begin by making a beehive using the bubble wrap. Cut out an appropriate beehive and paint it. To ensure the paint sticks to the bubble wrap, add PVA glue to ready-mixed paint. Now make some bees to fly in and around the beehive by rolling card into a tube, painting it brown and yellow and adding tissue paper wings. Print a flower border around the base of the display area using the found materials and attach the beehive to the wall. Add pieces of Velcro to each bee and to different places on the display for the bees to rest. Encourage the children to move the bees around to different parts of the display using positional language to describe where they are placing them – for example, 'This bee is going on top of a flower', 'This bee is going in between/next to these other bees' and so on.

Support
Work closely with the children as they place the bees, directing them using positional language.

Extension
Make instruction cards for the children to follow that give a sequence of different positions for the bees to be placed in.

Encourage the children to work collaboratively, giving instructions to each other as to where to place the bees on the display.

Learning objective
To use everyday words to describe position.

Group size
Small groups of no more than four children.

Home links
Ask parents and carers to stress positional language when putting away shopping or tidying up with their children.

This shell, that shell

Learning objective
To sort using given and own criteria.

Group size
Small groups of up to four children.

What you need

Sand tray; selection of different-sized and different-shaped shells and other seaside objects such as seaweed, feathers and pebbles, all natural materials from an existing collection; lollipop sticks; card; writing and drawing materials.

Preparation

Bury the shells in the sand tray. Make labels by attaching pieces of card to the lollipop sticks.

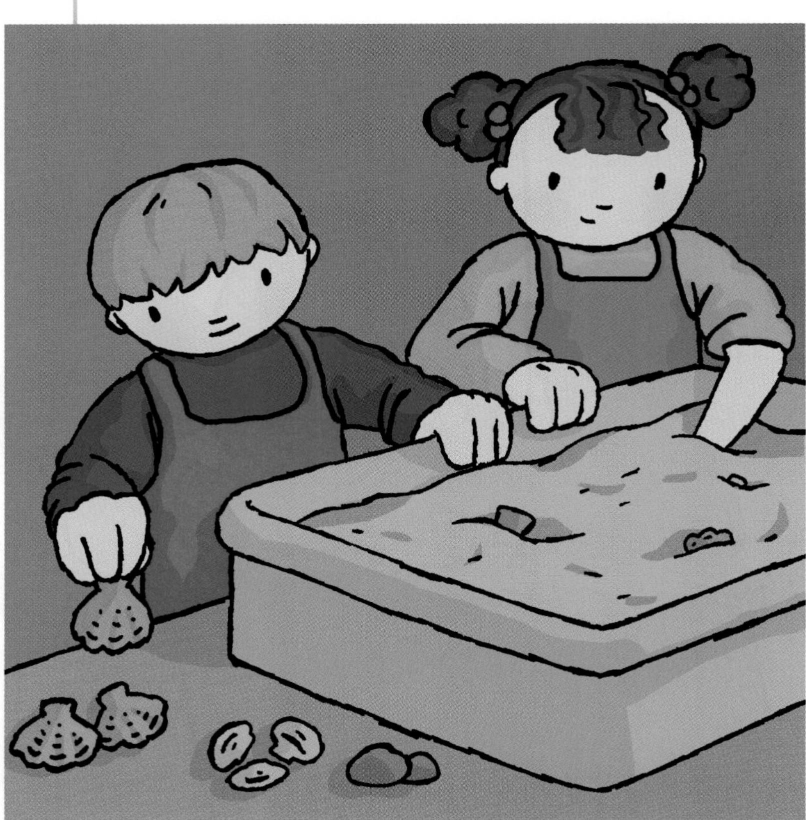

What to do

Explain to the children that hidden in the sand tray are different-shaped and different-sized shells which you would like them to find and sort into sets. Let them sift carefully through the sand and as they find the shells, ask them to place all the small ones together, the medium-sized ones together and the large ones together, and to write or draw labels to identify them. Suggest to the children other ways in which the shells could be sorted, for example: colour – place all the white or blue/black shells together; shape – place all the round shells together, and so on.

Create a story with the children based around a visit to the seaside on a hot summer's day. Choose a few children to share their own experiences with the group and ensure you incorporate these into your story. In turn, introduce the objects they may find on the beach, placing them in context and encouraging the children to name them.

Invite the children to sort and label the rest of the seaside items according to their own criteria.

Throughout the activity, encourage the use of mathematical language including number names, 'more', 'less', 'on', 'next to', 'under' and so on.

Support

Provide the children with a range of criteria to sort the seaside items to. Some children may need additional help to start the sorting process.

Extension

Ask the children to sort with two criteria, for example, shells which are round and small.

Use plastic boxes to add pools of water to the sand tray for the children to act out seaside scenes. Invite them to place different animals in their correct habitats.

Home links
Ask parents and carers to involve their children in everyday tasks that involve sorting, such as washing into colours, cutlery and glasses into cupboards, clothes into drawers and so on.

Which goes where?

What you need

A copy of the photocopiable sheet on page 70 for each child; scissors; glue; aprons; protective table covering; candle; candle holder; vase; flowers; lantern; tea light; writing and colouring materials.

Preparation

Cover a table with a protective cloth and ensure that all the children are wearing aprons. Through practical play activities, provide opportunities for the children to develop their matching skills.

What to do

Talk to the children about the festival of Wesak. Explain that during Wesak, people decorate their homes with lanterns and flowers.

Introduce the selection of objects to the children and encourage them to name each one. Ask them if they know what any of the objects are used for and if they have anything similar at home.

Encourage the children to count with you as you point to each object from your selection. Throughout this introductory activity, ask them questions such as, 'What does number 3 look like?', 'Can you draw it in the air or on your hand?', 'If we had one more flower, how many would we have altogether?', 'If we took one flower away, how many would be left behind?', 'Which object is between the candle and the vase?' and so on. Use positional language to ask the children to place the objects in different orders. For example, 'Place the tea light in front of the lantern'.

Now tell the children that some of the items could be paired together. Challenge them to say which ones and, if possible, to give reasons why.

Provide each of the children with a photocopiable sheet and ask them to match the items into pairs. Encourage them to colour the objects and draw lines between those that go together.

Support

Offer supervision to the children in matching the items together, or draw the lines on yourself for them to trace.

Extension

Ask the children to add labels to the items on their sheet.

Learning objective
To investigate numbers by discussing them and asking questions.

Group size
Small groups.

Home links
Ask parents and carers to visit a library with their children, or look through books at home, to find pictures of Buddha, which the children could bring to the setting to share with the group.

Pints of milk

Learning objective
In practical activities and discussion begin to use the vocabulary involved in adding and subtracting.

Group size
Any size.

What you need
Selection of dairy products; scissors; photocopiable sheet on page 71; paper; card; writing and drawing materials.

Preparation
Laminate the photocopiable sheet and cut around the milk bottles to make individual number cards.

What to do
Show the children the selection of dairy products and provide opportunities for a tasting session. Ask which products the children like best and why.

Explain that dairy products and honey are the traditional food eaten during Shavuot because they remind people of when there was very little meat to eat.

Provide each child with paper and ask them to draw and colour their favourite dairy product. Photocopy drawings where necessary so that you have several of each item. Trim the finished drawings, mount them on card and laminate them, then cut them out.

Lay the pictures on a table and ask the children to take turns collecting given numbers of products that are all the same, such as three pints of milk, then two pints of milk. Ask how many pints of milk they have when they put them all together. Combine different amounts to help reinforce the concept of addition.

When the children are confident with this, invite them to add together two sets of different products. Place the number cards face down and invite the children to turn them over to find out how many of each set they need. Encourage them to say what they are doing, for example, 'One pot of cream and two blocks of cheese makes a set of three dairy products'.

Throughout the activity, stress a range of vocabulary for addition, including 'plus', 'and', 'add', 'more than', 'altogether', 'next number', 'total' and so on.

Support
Invite the children just to turn the number cards and collect the given number of items.

Extension
Introduce subtraction to the children using relevant language such as 'take away', 'less' and 'how many left?'.

Home links
Invite parents and carers on a group visit to a farm, to see cows being milked and so on.

SUMMER FESTIVAL

Midsummer's Day

Tap those toes

Learning objective
To become aware of the passage of small amounts of time and ways to measure it.

Group size
Small groups.

What you need
One-minute sand timers; crêpe paper; sticky tape; scissors; 'happy' music; tape or CD player.

Preparation
Cut crêpe paper into long strips and use sticky tape to attach several colours together to act as streamers.

What to do
Explain to the children that Midsummer's day is a summer festival to celebrate the longest day of the year. Play the music to the children asking them to say how it makes them feel – happy or sad? Ask them to clap their hands in time to the music and when they are used to this, try keeping time with different parts of the body such as tapping their knees, stamping their feet, swaying and so on. Whenever necessary, remind the children to listen to and keep in time with the rhythm of the music.

Explain to the children they are going to clap with the music for one minute and that you will use a sand timer to measure this. Place the sand timer so that the children can see it as they clap, and tell them that when all the sand from the top half has run into the bottom half, one minute has passed. Ask the children to suggest other actions that they would like to perform together to the music for one minute.

Provide the children with the streamers and invite them to perform their own happy, 'summery' movements to the music. Tell them that you will time them and that each time a minute is up you will shout 'Change!' and they must find a different type of movement to perform, or change the direction of their movement. Remind them to look out all the time for those around them and to be careful not to bump into one another.

Support
Perform simple movements at all times for the children to follow.

Extension
Extend the activity by making the dance longer and more complex.

Home links
Ask parents and carers to point out different types of clocks to their children at home, and to look at hour times on traditional clock faces.

Shape up

Learning objectives
To use everyday words to describe position; to describe the shape and size of flat shapes.

Group size
Small groups.

What you need
A copy of the photocopiable sheet on page 72 for each child; scissors; colouring and writing materials; adhesive; A3 card; whiteboard.

Preparation
Ask the children to check the colour of their dad's (or other special male figure's) hair and eyes the day before you plan to do this activity.

What to do
Tell the children that Father's Day is a time when families show their appreciation to fathers and father figures, and that you are going to make cards to do this. Fold the A3 cards in half and write the words 'Happy Father's Day' at the top of each.

Provide each child with a photocopiable sheet and a folded card. On the whiteboard, demonstrate how to draw an oval, then help each child to draw a large oval on the front of their card underneath the words, explaining that this is going to be the face of their father, or chosen male figure. Ask them to colour in the shapes on the photocopiable sheet, choosing the appropriate colour for the eyes. As the children work, talk about the names of the shapes, asking questions such as, 'What shape is the mouth?', 'What is the triangle going to be?', 'What different shapes are the eyes made up of?' and so on.

When the children have finished colouring, help them to cut the shapes out and stick them in the correct positions on the card. Throughout the activity, encourage the use of positional language. For example, discuss which features go at the top of the oval, underneath the nose, above the eyes, on either side of the oval and so on.

Invite the children to draw on their fathers' hair, talking about how it goes at the top of the face (and at the bottom for any beards, and between the nose and the mouth for any moustaches!).

Support
Offer close supervision to the children in cutting and sticking features on their ovals, reinforcing the positional language as you help them, prompting them with questions. Write messages inside the cards for them to copy.

Extension
Invite the children to write independently their own messages inside their cards.

Home links
Ask male parents and carers to sit for their children to draw portraits of them at home, for the children to bring to the setting to make into a display.

SUMMER FESTIVAL

Dragon Boat Festival

The boat race

Learning objective
To recognize first, second and third.

Group size
Small groups of up to four children.

What you need
Paper; card; selection of reclaimed materials; straws; adhesive; sticky tape; scissors; whistle; pictures and models of boats; colouring materials; water trough; ribbon.

Preparation
Look at pictures and models of boats, naming the different parts. Discuss with the children how they could use junk materials to make a boat and to think about different ways of fixing a mast to their boat. Challenge them to make a boat using junk modelling materials, and emphasize that each boat needs a base, a mast and a flag with a dragon design.

Offer plenty of assistance in building the boats and draw simple examples of dragon designs for the children to copy onto their sails. Make a three-stepped platform numbered first, second and third for the end of the boat race.

What to do
This festival remembers how village people in China saved a drowned man's body from the water, where it might have been eaten by fish. Invite the children to name, show and talk about their boats. Discuss what a race is. Have they ever seen or been in one? What must someone do to win a race?

Explain to the children that they are going to race their boats in the water tray, to see whose will pass the winning line first, second and third. Demonstrate how to move the boats, by blowing or wafting paper.

Allow the children time to practise moving their boats before attaching the ribbon across the water tray to create a winning line. Choose a child to start the race by blowing the whistle. During the race, commentate using appropriate language such as 'first', 'next', 'last' and so on. When the race is finished, place the winning boat on the platform with second and third either side. Give three cheers for the winner!

Support
Make a selection of boats for the children to choose from.

Extension
Encourage the children to look at what may have made the winning boat most successful and to build an even better boat.

Home links
Ask parents and carers to experiment with making boats at bathtime, using fruit peel, old margarine tubs and so on.

O-bon

Ship shape

Learning objective
To discuss and compare the properties of solid and flat shapes.

Group size
Up to four children.

What you need
Card; polystyrene tiles; lolly sticks; colouring materials; scissors; sticky tape; water tray; aprons; 2D shapes.

Preparation
Fill the water tray and cut the polystyrene and card into different shapes such as square, circle, triangle and rectangle.

What to do
Explain that O-bon is a happy Japanese festival when the spirits of the ancestors are welcomed home on an annual visit. Spirits are guided on their way by floating tiny candles in paper boats on the river at night.

Introduce the selection of 2D shapes to the children and ask them to look for similarities and differences. Talk to them about the shapes. How many sides does each shape have? Are all the sides the same? Can the shape roll? Can they see any corners? Are any of the shapes similar?

Explain to the children that they are going to choose shapes to make their own boats and then find sails that are the same as one side of the shape, for example, a prism boat with a triangle sail. Invite them to decorate their boats and to name the shapes they are using as they do so. Help them to attach the sail to the boat with a lollipop stick.

Challenge the children to place several boats in the water tray and sort them into sets of shapes, then encourage them to sail all the same-shaped boats together.

Provide opportunities for the children to participate in boat races to see which shape makes the best sail. Can the children think of some different ways to make the boats move more efficiently?

Support
Guide the children in matching and attaching sails to boats. Advise them to concentrate on just the sails when sorting boats into sets.

Extension
Provide the children with a wider selection of more random shapes to make boats with.

Home links
Suggest that parents and carers accompany the children on a 'shape walk' around the local environment, or that they carry out a 'shape search' in and around the home.

Colourful bands

What you need

Coloured beads and strings; paper; glue; scissors; tissue paper; sequins; gummed paper; writing and colouring materials; hole-punch; treasury tags; stapler; sticky tape; tubs; protective table covering; aprons.

Preparation

Cut thin strips of paper about 2cm x 30cm. Arrange the selection of resources into labelled tubs and place these in the centre of a table covered with a protective cloth, along with the glue, sticky tape and scissors.

What to do

Explain to the children that Raksha means 'to protect' and that Bandhan means 'to tie', and that on this festival sisters tie a rakhi – a colourful bracelet – around their brothers' right wrists to protect them from evil. In return, brothers promise to look after their sisters in the coming year.

Introduce the strings and beads to the children, explaining that they are going to make rakhis for their friends. Invite each child to ask their friend what colours and patterns they might like on their rakhi. Discuss with the children how they are going to make the bracelets the correct length to fit their friends' wrists. Suggest that they could use the string to carefully measure around each other's wrists. When describing how to do this, use language such as 'short', 'shorter', 'long', 'longer', 'the right length', 'measure', 'size' and so on. Show the children how to keep their finger in place on the string and hold it next to the strips of paper. Mark where the string comes to for them, or offer guidance as they make the marks for each other. Once the strips have been cut to size, encourage the children to test the length around their friends' wrists.

Invite the children to decorate their strips of card in a colourful and interesting pattern. Then suggest that they punch holes into the strips and use a treasury tag to join the ends together.

Let the children repeat the activity to make bracelets to take home for brothers, sisters or special friends that are not at the setting. Explain that not all wrists are the same size, so to make the bracelets adjustable extra holes should be punched on either side of the bracelet.

Support

Pre-make a selection of different-sized strips for the children to test on each other's wrists to find the nearest size.

Extension

Encourage the children to try making a sequinned pattern on their bracelet. They could also measure the bracelets to find the longest using a non-standard unit of measure, such as a gummed square.

Learning objective
To use mathematical ideas and methods to solve practical problems of measurement.

Group size
Small groups.

Home links
Ask parents and carers to use non-standard units to measure things around the home, such as strides to measure rooms, or place mats to measure tables.

Janamashtami

Whose birthday?

Learning objectives
To recognize the names of the months of the year; to represent data pictorially.

Group size
Whole group.

What you need
Card; writing and drawing materials; paint; selection of small boxes; lolly sticks; scissors; glue; stapler; coloured backing paper; pictures of cradles.

Preparation
Staple backing paper to the wall; compile a list of the months in which the children's birthdays fall.

What to do
Explain that Janamashtami is a festival commemorating Krishna's birthday. Krishna was born at midnight and many people now stay up to greet the baby Krishna. A statue of the baby is placed in a decorated cradle so that people can file past and rock the cradle.

Introduce the months of the year to the children and encourage them to recite them. Ask the children to talk about what a birthday is and to tell you what month theirs falls in. Use your register to help those that are unsure and challenge all the children to try to remember their birthday months.

Explain to the children that they are going to make a cradle for each month of the year. Show them the pictures of cradles, discussing what they are used for.

Ask the children how many cradles will be needed. Make 12 cradles by sealing the small boxes and decorating them. Make small slits along the top edge of the box that the lolly stick will fit into and attach month labels to the front of the cradles. Invite each child to draw a picture of themselves on a piece of card and attach the pictures to the lolly sticks with the children's names on them. Ask the children to help you place the cradles in order. Explain to them that as you call out the name of each month, you would like all the children born in that month to place their lolly sticks in the cradle of their birthday month.

Once all the lolly sticks are placed, look at the cradles and count the birthdays in each month. Talk about which month has the most birthdays and point out any months that have none.

Support
Provide small photographs of the children for those that have trouble drawing small enough pictures of themselves.

Extension
Ask the children to find out which day of the week they were born on. This could then be incorporated into the display by labelling the lolly sticks with the corresponding days.

Home links
Ask the children to find out what months other members of their families were born in and add this information to the display.

Fallen leaves

Learning objective
To begin to use the vocabulary used in addition and subtraction in practical activities.

Group size
Groups of four children.

What you need

Card; colouring materials; a copy of the photocopiable sheet on page 73 for each child; dice; scissors; laminator or sticky-backed plastic.

Preparation

On the photocopiable sheets, colour the leaves in orange, pink, yellow, brown, green and red. Then colour the trees, laminate the sheets and cut out the leaves and the trees. Make coloured dice to match the leaves.

What to do

Provide each player with a tree and place the coloured leaves in the middle. Explain that the leaves have fallen from the trees and that the players will have to take turns to place the leaves back on the trees.

Before beginning the game, ask the children to suggest why the leaves have fallen and what colours they are. Tell them that they are to take turns to roll the dice and that they must pick up a leaf that matches the colour thrown. When all the leaves have been collected, the children should count the leaves on their tree – the winner is the one with the most leaves.

Whilst the tree is still full of leaves, reverse the operation so that this time when the dice is rolled, the child takes away the correct coloured leaf. The winner is the child who removes the last leaf. Introduce the language of subtraction by asking the children questions such as, 'How many red leaves are left on the tree?', 'Which colour has the smallest number of leaves on the tree?' and so on.

Throughout this activity, talk about the changes that take place through the seasons. Are the trees in the environment all the same? Look for and talk about different shapes, sizes and colours. Discuss with the children the different parts of a tree: the trunk, bark, roots, branches, twigs, buds and so on.

Support

Limit the number of colours and leaves that the children use.

Extension

Add numbers to the leaves and dice rather than colouring them.

Home links
Ask parents and carers to collect fallen leaves and bark with their children to take prints and make rubbings.

When the wind blows

Learning objective
To sequence items in numbered order.

Group size
Any size groups

What you need

The Wind Blew by Pat Hutchins (Red Fox); props based on the story, such as a scarf, balloon, umbrella, newspaper, kite and so on; pictures of characters from the story; card; writing materials.

Preparation

Draw the characters from the story in your own style on card and colour them in. Place the various items owned by the different characters in the story into a sack or box. Make a large number line to 11, draw a box underneath each number labelled first, second, third and so on.

What to do

Read *The Wind Blew* to the children and ask them to listen out for the items that blew away and to which characters they had belonged.

Introduce the language of ordinal numbers by placing a group of children in a line and asking the first child to pick up a specific prop, then the second child and so on. When the children have completed this, ask the others to say what the first child is holding, what object the fourth child is holding, and so on.

Encourage the children to take turns to choose an object from the sack or box and to place it with the picture of the appropriate character.

Read the story a second time so that the children can check that they have matched the items to the characters correctly. As each item is mentioned this time, choose a child and ask him or her to place it under the number line in the correct box.

Support

Attach a number card to each item so that the children can match it to the number line.

Extension

Invite the children to place the items in the correct boxes on the number line from memory. More confident children could volunteer to take turns reading lines from the story with you.

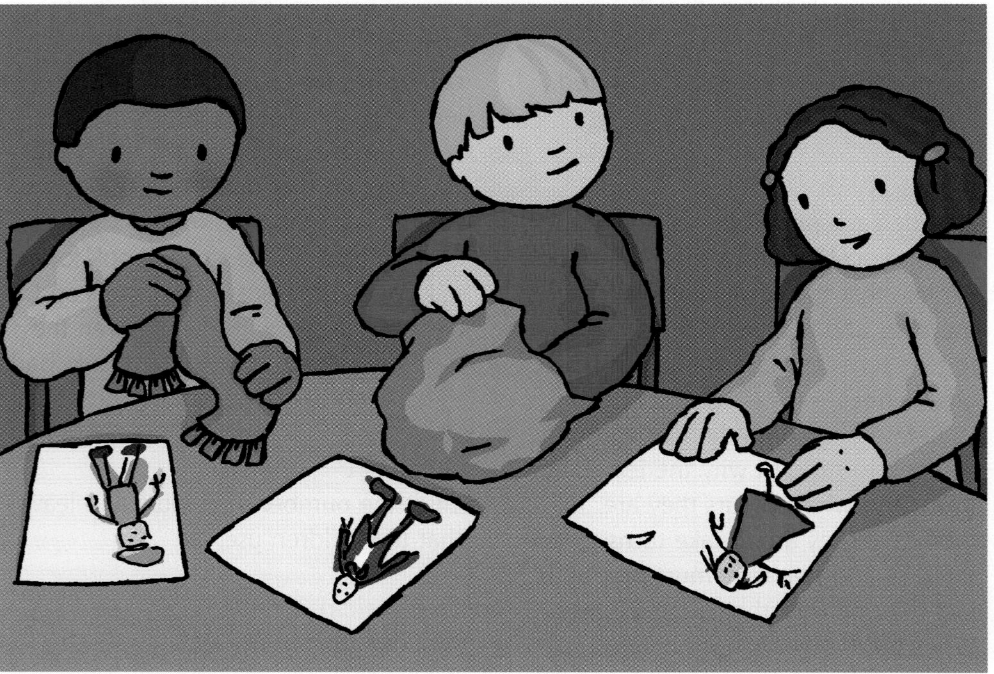

Home links
Ask parents and carers to take their child for a walk on a windy day to make observations about the noise and feel of the wind and the effect it has on the trees and so on.

Crack a conker

Learning objectives
To use language such as 'bigger' and 'smaller' to compare and order items; to count reliably up to ten everyday objects.

Group size
Small groups

What you need
An enlarged laminated copy of the photocopiable sheet on page 74; selection of conkers; A4 paper; writing materials.

What to do
Read the poem to the children and discuss what it is about. Read it again to see if their ideas were correct and to familiarize them with it.

Give each child a piece of paper and pencil or pen and explain that you will read the poem a third time, and that you would like them all to make a mark on their paper each time somebody has a go at trying to hit the conker. When the poem is finished, ask the children to tell you how many marks they have made. Did everybody make the same number of marks?

Introduce your selection of conkers and challenge the children to sort them into a variety of categories such as big, little, round, flat-edged, shiny and so on. Tell the children that you are slowly going to count up how many conkers are in each set while they make a mark for each one that you count. After counting all the sets, ask the children to check that they have made the right number of marks.

Using the information that has been gathered, demonstrate to the children how it can be organized in different ways, for example: pictograms (where the children draw pictures of conkers to display in a chart); block graphs (squares of coloured paper stuck vertically or horizontally to represent each of the conkers in a given set); simple illustrated sets of conkers showing how many belong to each set, and so on.

When the different graphs/charts have been completed, encourage the children to use them to retrieve information. Ask simple questions such as, 'Are there more small conkers or big conkers?', 'Which set has the most conkers?', and encourage the children to answer them by referring to the various charts.

Support
Work one-to-one with the children in counting the conkers.

Extension
Encourage the children to create their own version of one of the charts. Let them colour and label their charts and display them with the enlarged poem.

Home links
Ask parents and carers to take their children on an autumn walk to collect fallen conkers, which could be used for the activity.

Helicopters

Learning objectives
To count in order; to measure short periods of time.

Group size
Any size.

What you need

Card; writing materials; sycamore wings, enough for each child; open space; climbing frame or platform; first-floor window.

Preparation

Show the children how to throw sycamore wings upwards so that they twirl to the floor, and let them practise throwing the wings themselves. Cut large sycamore wing shapes from card, one for each child.

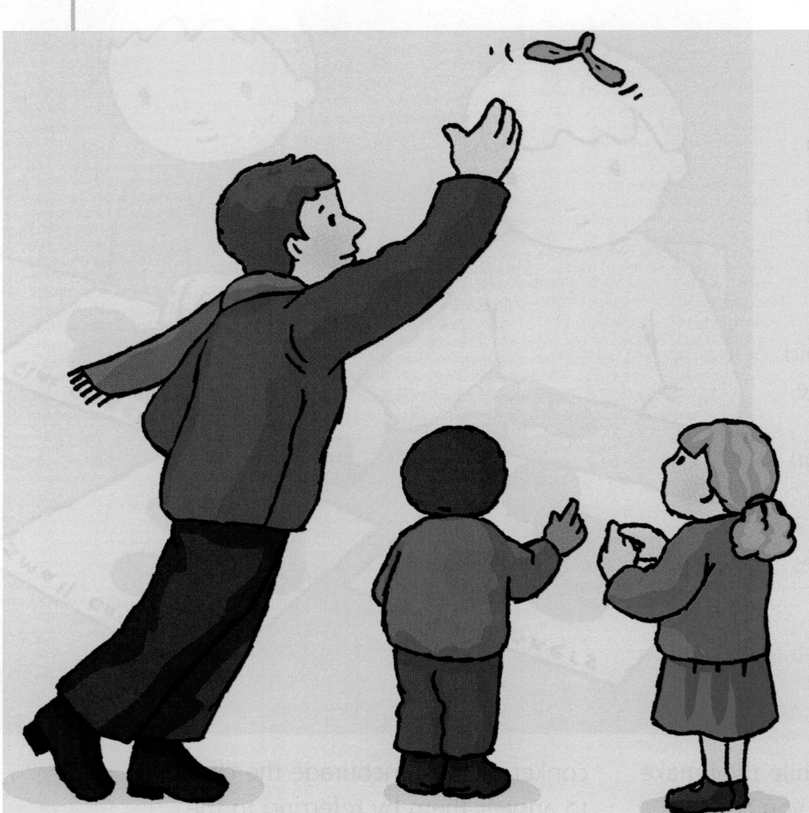

What to do

Hand out the real sycamore wings and explain to the children that they are going to have a race to see whose takes the longest time to fall to the ground. Ask the children for suggestions as to how to make the competition fair and discuss the need to all start together. Now ask a few children to throw the wings up and watch them fall to the ground. Ask them to shout out their name as soon as their sycamore wing hits the ground.

Explain to the children that now you will throw the sycamore wing from three different heights and you would like them to time how long it takes for it to reach the ground each time by counting. Practise counting seconds with the children by saying, 'One banana, two bananas...' and so on. Gather the children as you throw the sycamore wing, first from standing on the ground, then from a slightly increased height, such as a raised platform or climbing frame, and finally from an even greater height, such as a first floor window with the children below you. Each time, encourage the children to count steadily and stop when the sycamore wing has reached the ground. Make a note of each length of time taken in number of seconds and ask the children to record these times themselves onto their sycamore-shaped pieces of card.

Support

Invite the children to just focus on the throwing aspect of the activity and record the three lengths of time just by shortest, medium and longest.

Extension

Encourage the children to look at standard units of measure by using a simple timer.

Home links
Ask parents and carers to time their children carrying out simple activities around the home, to develop their concept of different time periods.

Let's go fly a kite

What you need
Plastic bags; muslin; tracing paper; glue; scissors; paper; string; hole-punch; sticky tape; aprons; protective table covering; writing, drawing and painting materials.

Preparation
Cover a table with a protective cloth and ensure that all the children are wearing aprons. Cut out kite shapes in different sizes from the plastic bags, muslin and tracing paper. Cut pieces of string to attach to the kite (approximately 1m long) and cut small pieces of paper into symmetrical shapes.

What to do
Explain to the children that windy days are excellent for flying kites. Tell them that they are going to make kites with their friends. Show the children the selection of pre-cut paper shapes and ask them to describe the shapes using appropriate mathematical language. Fold the shapes in half to demonstrate how each side is exactly the same. Invite the children to make kites that are decorated symmetrically. Show them how to do this by gluing the paper shapes onto exactly the same place on each side of the kite.

Organize the children into pairs to work on their kites. When they have finished, make a hole with the hole-punch in the base of each kite, reinforce it with sticky tape and attach the length of string. Test the kites outside on a windy day by running with them.

Support
To familiarize the children with the concept of symmetry, make butterflies by painting two wings on one half of a piece of paper, then folding it to make four wings.

Extension
Introduce the children to the use of mirrors as a way of completing an image in exact symmetry. Encourage them to experiment with different lines of symmetry on pictures and photographs to see how it changes them. They could also investigate what their faces look like if they place the mirror down the centre. Explain that nobody's face is exactly symmetrical.

Learning objective
To show an awareness of symmetry in 2D shapes.

Group size
Small groups in pairs.

Home links
Ask parents and carers to look with their children for symmetrical shapes or patterns at home.

Baskets of fruit

Learning objectives
To use the language of size; to use developing mathematical ideas and methods to solve practical problems.

Group size
Small groups in pairs.

What you need

Ingredients for play dough (flour, salt, water, oil, cream of tartar, food colouring in autumn fruit colours); selection of fresh autumn fruit, such as apples, blackberries and pears; selection of different-sized baskets; knife (adult use).

Preparation

Make batches of play dough in autumn fruit colours by mixing one cup of flour, half a cup of water, one tablespoon of oil, half a cup of salt, one teaspoon of cream of tartar and one teaspoon of food colouring in a pan over a low heat. Stir until the dough solidifies, tip out of the pan and knead until smooth.

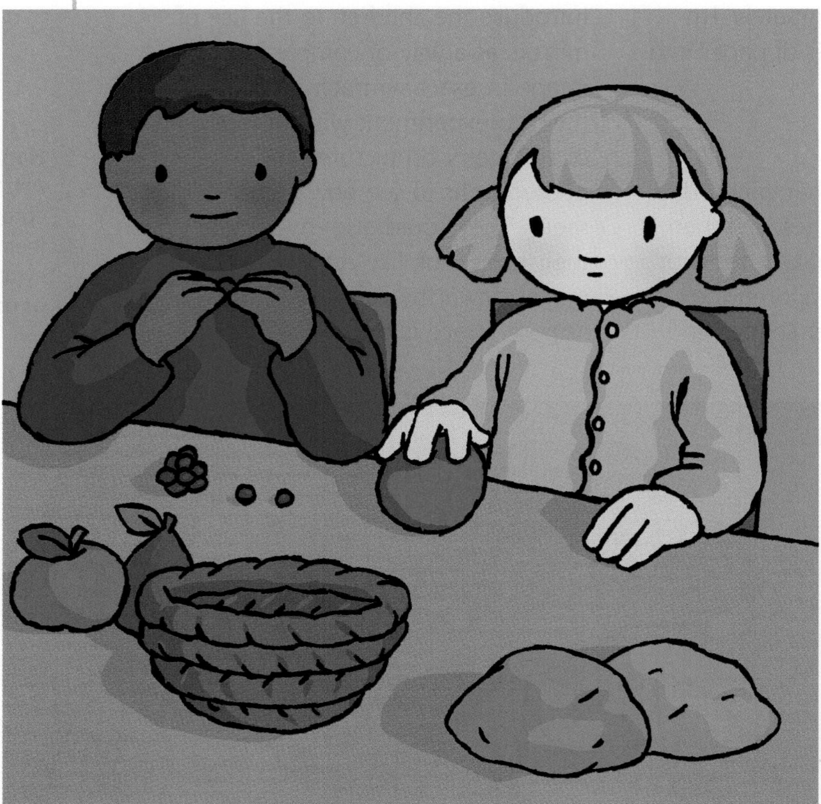

What to do

Show the children the baskets and the selection of fresh fruit. Discuss the colour, shape and size of each different type of fruit. Ask questions such as, 'Is it round?', 'Does it roll?', 'Is it big or little?', 'Is it fat or thin?' and so on. Let the children hold the fruit as they talk about it. Cut some of the fruit open and look at its flesh and seeds.

Challenge the children to estimate how many pieces of one particular fruit will fill the basket. Repeat with each of the different types of fruit and ask the children to explain reasons for their estimations. They should be thinking about the size and shape of each piece of fruit.

Explain to the children that they are going to use the play dough to make a basket of their own for their friend to fill with play dough fruit. The children should work together to estimate how much of a particular fruit will fill the basket, considering the issues of size and shape. The second child should now make the fruit and fill the basket, to see if their estimation was correct.

Support

Help the children to count the pieces of fruit as they add them to the baskets, rather than letting them make estimations.

Extension

Challenge the children to record both their estimations and the actual amounts to see how good they were at predicting the numbers.

Home links
Ask parents and carers to estimate the ratio of items to packaging with their children when they are out shopping, for example, 'How many biscuits are there in the packet?' or 'How many apples will fill the bag?'.

AUTUMN FESTIVAL

Grandparent's Day

Whose hand is it?

What you need
An A3 copy of the photocopiable sheet on page 75; photographs of the children's grandparents; paint; paintbrushes or sponges; warm water; paper towels; soap; paper; aprons; protective table covering.

Preparation
Ask parents and carers to provide photographs of the children's grandparents. Cover a table and place the paints in the centre. Help the children to put on aprons.

What to do
Look together at the photographs of the grandparents and look at similarities and differences between their physical features. Tell the children that on 'Grandparent's Day' we think about our grandmothers and grandfathers. Discuss with the children who grandparents are and what the relationship is between the children's own parents and grandparents. Use the photographs to develop the children's language about size and colour. Discuss who is the tallest and shortest and who has brown, grey, blonde hair and so on.

Now order the children into size, from tallest to shortest. Ask them questions that encourage them to make comparisons, such as, 'Has the tallest child got the tallest grandparent?', 'Has the tallest child got the longest feet?', 'Has the smallest child got the smallest hand span?' and so on. Challenge the children to guess at answers before testing them out.

Explain to the children that they are going to make a family tree out of handprints, showing their immediate family and their grandparents. Discuss which members of the family they will need to add to their tree. Help them to paint their hand and make a print for each family member. When the handprints are dry, write the people's names on them.

Finally, ask the children to glue the prints onto the tree outline on the enlarged photocopiable sheet.

Support
Invite the children to concentrate on making just enough handprints for each of their grandparents.

Extension
Encourage the children to add other family members to their tree, such as cousins, aunts and uncles.

Learning objective
To order pictures of people into sets using the language of size and colour.

Group size
Small groups.

Home links
Ask parents and carers to send in photographs for the children to add to their family tree.

Favourite part of the day

Learning objective
To become familiar with the language of time.

Group size
Small groups.

What you need

Large sheets of paper; selection of paints; paintbrushes; collage materials; adhesive; spatulas; water; scissors; paper for mounting; protective table covering and aprons; props to represent different times of the day such as blanket, towel, toothbrush, plate, knife and fork, dressing gown and so on.

Preparation

Cover the table with a protective cloth and help the children to put on aprons. Place the paints and collage materials in the middle of the table.

What to do

Explain to the children that Yom Kippur is a Jewish festival, lasting 24 hours, when members of Jewish families say sorry to each other.

Discuss with the children the names for the different parts of the day – morning, afternoon and evening – and ask them to suggest things that typically happen at each of these times. Use the props and some of the children to re-enact activities from throughout the day. Encourage the use of time language, including words such as 'next', 'after', 'morning', 'before', 'later', 'afternoon', 'evening' and so on.

Ask the children to decide what their favourite time of the day is and encourage them to give reasons why.

Now suggest that the children paint or collage their favourite time of the day. Remind them to add something to their picture which will clearly show the time of the day, such as a sun, or closed curtains, moon and stars, and so on. When the pictures are completed, mount and place them in order on a display board with a relevant caption alongside each one.

Support

Invite the children to concentrate on activities that only take place in the morning and afternoon.

Extension

Use a large clock to introduce o'clock times and display a relevant time with each of the pictures.

Home links
Ask each child to discover their parent or carer's favourite time of the day. This information could be used to make simple charts to compare their findings.

In and out

What you need

Card; paper; large piece of fabric; tissue or crêpe paper in a selection of colours; scissors; sticky tape; climbing or playhouse frame; sticky tape; writing and drawing materials.

Preparation

Cover the frame with the fabric to create a covered area that the children can move in and out of.

What to do

Explain to the children that a long time ago, when the Jews travelled through the wilderness, they constructed huts called sukkahs to shelter themselves.

Ask for the children's assistance in transforming the climbing frame into a sukkah. Let them help you to drape fabric over it and explain that you would now like to decorate it with flower garlands. Invite the children to make leaves and flowers with the tissue and crêpe paper. Attach the flowers into long garlands using sticky tape and arrange them over the sukkah.

When the sukkah has been decorated, let the children play in it. Develop their positional language by offering instructions for them to follow, such as, 'Crawl into the sukkah', 'Walk behind the sukkah', 'Jump around the sukkah', 'Stand next to the sukkah' and so on.

When the children are familiar with this, develop the activity by giving them a list of instructions to carry out in a particular order.

Support

Support the children by moving with them, perhaps holding their hands, explaining the meaning of the different positional words.

Extension

Provide the children with two or more instructions to follow.

Alternatively, use the sukkah as a scene for playing listening and guessing games. One child should sit inside the sukkah and another child stand behind it to guess who is in the sukkah by listening carefully to the voice. Develop this further by introducing musical instruments for the children to play and guess.

Learning objective
To observe and use positional language.

Group size
Small groups.

Home links
Provide parents and carers with a list of vocabulary related to positional language to use at home with their children.

Ladle the soup

Learning objectives
In practical activities and discussion begin to use the vocabulary involved in adding and subtracting; to begin to recognize coins and their value.

Group size
Up to four children.

What you need
Water tray; ladles; plastic bowls and baskets; selection of vegetables; play money; aprons; writing and drawing materials.

Preparation
Fill the water tray and ensure that all the children are wearing aprons.

What to do
Explain to the children that it is during harvest time that the farmer collects the food from the fields. Tell them that as it is a cold day, you are going to make these crops into harvest soup!

Introduce your selection of vegetables and look carefully at their size, colour and shape. Peel and chop the vegetables, counting the number of pieces, and place them in baskets for the children to buy in order to make the soup. Help the children to decide on an appropriate price for each type of vegetable piece and make price tags to display with the vegetables.

Tell the children that they are going to make soup by buying real vegetable pieces and placing them in the water tray. Now provide the children with play money with which to buy the vegetables. During this, ask questions such as, 'How many pieces of carrot have you bought?', 'Are there more peas than pieces of carrot?', 'If you buy two more pieces of carrot, how many will you have?', 'If you put one cabbage leaf back, how many will you have?' 'Can you count how many types of vegetable there are altogether?', 'How much money will a small bowl of soup cost?' and so on.

As an alternative to real vegetables, you can use plastic play vegetables or objects such as cubes and sponges.

Support
Price all the vegetables at 1p per piece to simplify the addition.

Extension
Make each type of vegetable a different price and use greater values.

Home links
Suggest to parents and carers that they make soup at home with their children.

Aim, fire!

Learning objectives
To find the total number of items in two groups by counting all of them; to use the vocabulary involved in adding and subtracting in practical activities and discussion.

Group size
Small groups.

What you need

A copy of the photocopiable sheet on page 76 for each child; scissors; glue; colouring, writing and drawing materials; paper; two large tins; card; small whiteboards and markers; number cards up to 5; protective table covering; aprons.

Preparation

Make arrows by rolling up paper into long thin tubes and attaching a cone-shaped arrowhead made from a semicircle of card. Cover the two large tins with brown paper to make the quivers. Put a protecting cover on the table and help the children to put on the aprons.

What to do

Explain to the children that the festival of Navaratri celebrates the victory of Rama over the demon king Ravana, whom Rama killed using arrows from his quiver.

Lay the number cards face down and ask a child to begin the activity by turning one of the cards over. Look at the number shown and count this amount of arrows into one of the quivers. Ask another child to turn a card over and place this number of arrows into the second quiver. With the children, count the arrows in each quiver separately first, then together to find the total.

Encourage the children to compare the amounts in the quivers. Lead them in counting both the smaller and the greater amount first when counting the quivers together.

Give each child a copy of the photocopiable sheet and invite them to cut out the arrows and stick the correct number of arrows onto each quiver.

Support

Invite the children to draw lines on the photocopiable sheet from the correct number of arrows to each quiver, rather than cutting them out.

Extension

Ask the children to keep a note of the number of arrows in each quiver and their combined total each time. Help them to write out these figures as addition sums.

Home links
Ask parents and carers to sort into sets and count toys with their children.

Let there be light

Learning objective
To use developing mathematical ideas and methods to solve practical problems.

Group size
Small groups.

What you need

Four sets of different-sized, -shaped and -coloured candles; writing and drawing materials; four large pieces of coloured card; scissors.

Preparation

Cut out four large candle templates in different shapes and sizes to sort the candles onto.

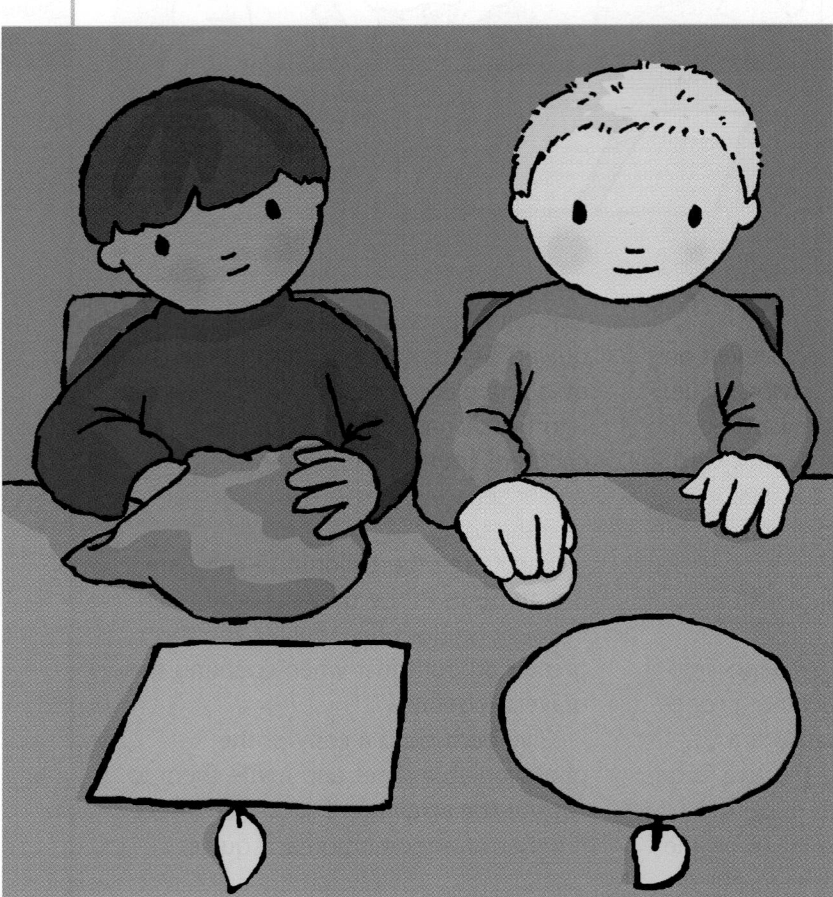

What to do

Explain to the children that the Hindu festival of Divali is a festival of light when people light candles or small clay lamps called divas in their homes. Introduce a range of mathematical language by telling the children a simple story about a Hindu child who wanted to buy a special candle for his mum.

Tell them that when he reached the shop, he found so many different candles that he did not know which to buy. Ask the children to suggest shapes and sizes that the candles might have come in, such as tall, thin, coloured and so on.

Tell the children that eventually the boy bought a variety of candles to bring home for his mum so that she could choose her favourite to light for Divali.

Produce a bag containing the selection of candles and explain that you would like the children to take turns to pick a candle out, describe it and place it on a candle template. Continue in this manner until each set of candles is on a different-coloured template.

As you carry out the activity, ask the children questions such as, 'How many thin candles are there?', 'How many fat red candles are there?' and so on. Write labels to identify the characteristics of each set.

Support

Limit the number, shape, size and colour of the candles to simplify the activity. Prompt the children with size and shape words when they are identifying the different types of candle.

Extension

Ask the children to look for candles with characteristics that apply to more than one set, such as tall, red candles and tall, blue candles, or green, round candles and green, triangular ones.

Home links
Ask parents and carers to make secret messages for their children by writing a word with hot candle wax. The child should shade over the paper with a felt-tipped pen or paint to reveal the secret message.

Round and round we go

What you need

Black paper; selection of colouring materials such as chalks, pastels, paints, crayons, colouring pencils; crêpe paper; glue; glitter; sequins; pictures of exploding fireworks; protective table covering; aprons.

Preparation

Make a Catherine wheel with the children by twisting strips of crêpe paper into a rope effect and by gluing these into a spiral shape on black paper.

What to do

Show the children the pictures of exploding fireworks and ask them what patterns they can see. Encourage them to describe the patterns, looking at their colour and shape. Discuss whether the pattern is recurring or not and what this means.

Invite the children to decorate their own Catherine wheels with patterns coming from the centre. Demonstrate how the different materials could be used to create a pattern, and provide opportunities for the children to make their own firework patterns. Encourage them to create different patterns.

Introduce a range of shapes, such as triangles, circles and rectangles, for the children to decorate with patterns. Encourage them to use glitter and sequins on their pictures to make them really dazzling.

These pictures could then be made into a firework display by mounting them onto a black background. Help the children to think of appropriate names with which to label their fireworks, such as 'Zooming triangle treat' or 'Spectacular circle'.

Support

Invite the children to practise making simple patterns by placing counters on squared paper.

Extension

Provide a range of collage materials for the children to create a repeating pattern with.

Learning objective
To talk about, recognize and re-create simple patterns.

Group size
Any size.

Home links
Display the children's Catherine wheels along with emergent writing describing the sounds and patterns of the fireworks. Invite parents and carers to provide Bonfire Night photographs to add to the display.

Make eight

Learning objectives
To separate a group of objects in different ways and begin to recognize that the total is still the same; to begin to relate addition to combining two groups of objects.

Group size
Up to four children.

What you need
Sand tray; eight small candles; picture of a menorah; whiteboards ; writing materials.

Preparation
Dampen the sand in the tray and place the candles nearby.

What to do
Explain to the children that Hanukkah is an eight-day Jewish festival at which candles are lit each day on a menorah. Introduce the picture of the menorah to the children and encourage them to count the candles. Ask questions such as, 'How many candles are on each side?', 'How many candles are there altogether?', 'If two were lit, how many candles would be unlit?' and so on.

Show the children the real candles and count them together. Explain that you would like them to press the candles into the damp sand on their sides in the same pattern that they are in on the menorah.

When the children have finished, talk about and try out different patterns that the candles could be placed in. Think about splitting the candles into different groups, such as five together and three together.

Draw rings around each group and record the totals in the sand, before smoothing it over to try a different combination. Reiterate that no matter how the candles are arranged, there are still only eight.

Support
Make marks in the damp sand for the children to follow when they are placing the candles.

It may be beneficial to use a selection of coloured candles so that the children can identify the number bonds clearly by looking at the sets of colours – for example, three red candles and five blue candles make eight candles altogether.

Extension
Provide the children with wipe-clean whiteboards and ask them to record their findings pictorially, practising different number bonds to 10.

Encourage the children to write the numbers in the sand themselves.

Home links
Ask parents and carers to practise combining and dividing groups of objects with their children at home.

Slime time

What you need
Soap flakes; warm water; shallow tray; selection of plastic cake decorations; kitchen tools such as tongs, fish slice, colander and so on; protective table covering; aprons; warm water; soap and paper towels.

Preparation
Cover the table and make the slime by gradually mixing soap flakes with warm water until they have dissolved. Add the plastic decorations to the slime. Ensure that all the children are wearing aprons. Check for soap allergies.

What to do
Explain to the children that the slime represents the snow and that unfortunately all the decorations have become lost in it. Challenge the children to guess how many decorations are hidden and record the children's estimations. Ask them to use the kitchen tools to find the decorations. As the decorations are found, the children should count them. During the activity, ask questions such as, 'How many more do you think are left?', 'If you find one more, how many will you have?', 'What is the next number?', 'What was the last number?', 'Which is the easiest tool to use to pick them up?', 'Who has found the most/fewest decorations?' and so on.

When all the decorations have been removed from the slime ask the children to group them according to similarities and then add the groups together, for example, 'Two snowmen and one fir tree makes three decorations in all'. Practical subtraction could also be introduced by posing problems such as, 'If there are four reindeer in the snow and one gets lost, how many are left?'.

Support
Show the children the decorations before hiding them in the snow, so that they know what and how many to look for.

Use fewer decorations and provide the children with a pictorial chart showing each one, so that they can cross off the pictures as the decorations are found.

Extension
Ask the children to stop at different points during the activity to record their findings so far by organizing the decorations they have found into illustrated sets. They could go on to use addition, subtraction and equals signs to turn their drawings into simple sums.

Learning objectives
To count reliably up to ten everyday objects; to begin to relate addition to combining two groups of objects and subtraction to 'taking away'.

Group size
Groups of up to four children.

Home links
Ask parents and carers to count decorations on their Christmas trees at home, as well as presents underneath it, mince pies on a plate and so on.

Big, bigger, biggest

Learning objective
To use language such as greater, smaller, heavier or lighter to compare quantities.

Group size
Any size.

What you need
Selection of winter clothes in different sizes, such as hats, scarves, gloves, wellington boots and so on; card; writing materials.

Preparation
Prepare labels for displaying with the clothes, including 'long', 'longer', 'longest', 'big', 'bigger', 'biggest' and so on.

What to do
Sing and play 'Here we go round in winter time' to the tune of 'Here We Go Round the Mulberry Bush' with the children. Perform the actions to the following verses:

This is the way we put on our scarf...
This is the way we pull on our hat...
This is the way we put on our gloves...
This is the way we pull on our wellies...

Ask the children if an adult would wear the same-sized hat, scarf and gloves as a child, and if not, why not? Show the children the different lengths of scarves and ask them who would wear which one. Encourage them to place these in order on the floor into long, longer and longest, stressing the appropriate vocabulary.

Take the other items and place them in turn in a comparative sequence, again stressing the correct vocabulary, for example, for gloves: wide, wider, widest; for hat: big, bigger, biggest and for wellington boots: large, larger, largest.

Support
Invite the children to make comparisons between just two objects, for example, 'bigger' and 'smaller'.

Extension
Encourage the children to measure the items using non-standard units and to make a written record of their results, for example, 'The gloves are ten thumb-widths wide'.

Alternatively, invite the children to record the rhyme onto tape. Type out the rhyme, adding the children's illustrations before laminating it. This could be used to read from when listening to the tape.

Home links
Ask parents and carers to look with their children at the different-sized clothes within their family. Could these be ordered? When helping the children to dress parents and carers could help them to think about the order in which clothes are worn.

Gorgeous gifts

What you need

Selection of different papers, including tissue and crêpe paper; Christmas wrapping paper; selection of boxes and containers; reclaimed materials; collage materials including ribbon; examples of small gifts such as bracelets, plastic cups, soft toys and so on; glue; scissors; sticky tape; split-pin fasteners; hole-punch; treasury tags; protective table covering; aprons.

Preparation

Cover the table and help the children to put on aprons. Arrange the selection of materials in the middle of the table.

What to do

Show the children the selection of gifts and explain that you would like them to find a box or a container for each gift so that it fits into it. Discuss the size and shape of a gift of your choice; will you need a round or a square box? Will it have to be short or tall? Wide or thin? To continue to reinforce the language of shape and size, ask 'silly' questions about the boxes, such as, 'Would an elephant fit in this little box?'.

Allow each child to choose a gift and to place it inside a suitable box. Encourage them to decorate the box using the paper and collage materials. Discuss different ways in which the gift box could be fastened. These could include: tying with ribbon; punching holes and threading through treasury tags; using sticky tape, glue or split-pin fasteners, and so on.

When the gifts are complete, arrange them on a table-top display.

Support

Provide plenty of assistance to the children with matching the gift to the correct size of box.

Extension

Encourage the children to carefully cut out wrapping paper, wrap the gift boxes with it and tie lengths of ribbon around it.

Learning objectives
To show curiosity and observation by talking about shapes, how they are the same or why some are different; to adapt shapes or cut material to size.

Group size
Any size.

Home links
Ask parents and carers to look carefully at packaging when they are shopping with their children and to discuss why there are different-sized containers for the same product, such as different-sized boxes of tea-bags and different-sized tins of beans.

All bare

Learning objective
To count up to five objects from a larger group of objects.

Group size
Up to four children.

What you need
Sand tray; selection of bare winter twigs; dry leaves; number cards up to 5.

Preparation
Place the twigs, leaves and branches close to the sand tray.

What to do
Show the children the number cards as they count with you to five. Now introduce the children to the twigs and count how many there are. Choose a child to pick a number card and to place the specified amount of twigs in the sand. Do this again, asking a child to arrange the same number of twigs but in a different formation.

Throughout the activity, question the children to ascertain their level of understanding. For example, ask them, 'Which group has more/less?', 'Can you count them?', 'Which group is easier to count?' and so on.

Repeat the activity, generating new numbers each time. The purpose of this exercise is for the children to understand that no matter how the twigs are arranged, the number of twigs that they are working with always remains the same.

Introduce the children to the collection of dry leaves. Invite them to place one leaf on each of the twigs and count how many leaves there are altogether. Extend this by asking them to match different numbers of leaves to the twigs. Ask the children to count the twigs and the leaves separately and then work out how many more leaves there are than twigs each time.

Support
Start the activity using just two twigs and encourage the children to work with an increasing number of twigs as they become more confident.

Extension
Encourage the children to use up to ten twigs and to match larger numbers of leaves to each twig. Start to use language such as, 'Three leaves with each twig will give us three times more leaves than twigs'.

Home links
Invite parents and carers to go for a walk with their children and to point out winter trees to them, looking for fallen leaves and noting the patterns of the branches against the sky.

Light it up

What you need
Four copies of the photocopiable sheet on page 77; colouring materials in red, blue, green and yellow; scissors.

Preparation
Colour the dominoes so that all matching shapes are the same colour, but different on each sheet, for example, all the triangles on one sheet will be blue, all the triangles on the next sheet will be red, and so on. Laminate the sheets and cut the dominoes out.

What to do
Talk to the children about how much more darkness there is in winter than in summer. Show them the dominoes and discuss how we use lights when it is dark. Discuss different types of light and how we use them, such as street lamps, torches, lamps on miners' hats, candles on special occasions and so on.

Look at the dominoes with the children and talk about the different types of light that are featured on them.

Give each of the children a different domino and lay the rest on the floor. Ask the children to tell the rest of the group about the shape, size and colour of their domino and then to find one from those laid out on the floor which has one similar attribute – either a matching colour or shape. Repeat this activity asking the children to find a domino with the same-coloured shape.

Share the dominoes among the children and explain that they are going to use them to play a game. The object of the game is to use all seven dominoes as soon as possible, matching up one attribute at a time. If a child is unable to go, the next child takes their turn and the first to use all their dominoes wins the game.

Support
Invite the children to play simple matching games with the dominoes. Each domino could be cut in half so that they can all be paired up, or pairs could be made by matching just half of each domino.

Extension
Add combinations of spots from one to five to the dominoes, and ask the children to match to match the numbers as well as, or instead of, colours and shapes.

Learning objectives
To use developing mathematical ideas and methods to solve practical problems; to recognize and match 2D shapes.

Group size
Groups of four children.

Home links
Ask parents and carers to play number dominoes and simple card games with their children at home.

Winter nuts

Learning objective
To find one more or one less than a number from 1 to 10; to use language such as more or less to compare two numbers.

Group size
Any size.

What you need
A variety of nuts in their shells, such as hazelnuts, walnuts and almonds; nutcracker; paper; pencils.

Preparation
Place the different nuts in separate containers. Draw and cut out a large outline of a hand.

What to do
Ask the children whether they know that you can buy nuts in their shells in winter. Look at the different nuts with them and show them how to crack some open. Name the different types of nut, discussing the variety of sizes, shapes and colours.

Tell the children that you would like them to try and pick up as many of a particular type of nut as they can in one hand. Before they do this, ask everyone to guess who will pick up the most nuts and why. Ask for suggestions as to how many this will be.

Encourage the children to take turns to pick up a handful of nuts and place them on the large hand outline so that they can be counted. Give the children paper and pencils with which to record the number they guessed, then ask them to write the actual number of nuts picked up next to it.

Continue this activity using all the different types of nut in turn. Ask questions comparing results, such as, 'Who was able to pick up the most nuts?', 'Who was able to pick up the smallest number of nuts?', 'Could you pick up more of the larger or smaller nuts? Why is this?' and so on.

Support
Leave out the recording of the amount of nuts. Reinforce the concepts through lots of practical activities.

Extension
Encourage the children to add together two handfuls of nuts (whether identical or not) to find the total. Alternatively, invite them to count out handfuls that have one more or one less nut than their first handful.

Home links
Ask parents and carers to count with their children, missing out numbers for them to fill in.

Whose house is next?

Learning objective
To order and follow a simple sequence.

Group size
Any size.

What you need
Large and small construction kits; sticky labels; writing materials; Father Christmas soft toy or play figure.

Preparation
Using the small construction kits, make a sleigh with the children for your Father Christmas to travel in.

What to do
Explain to the children that it is Christmas Eve and Father Christmas is going to deliver his presents. Ask them to make a row of houses using the construction equipment, for Father Christmas to visit in order.

Allow the children to work in pairs to build their house if they prefer. When they have finished, position the houses in two rows to make a street. Invite the children to number the houses using the sticky labels.

When the street is ready, send Father Christmas in his sleigh to deliver the presents to the houses in order. To assess the children's understanding of following a simple sequence, ask questions such as, 'Why does Father Christmas go to house number 4 after house number 3?', 'Which is the first house he will visit?', 'Which is the last house he will visit?' and so on.

To develop the activity further, make simple work cards, directing Father Christmas to certain houses, for example: 'Deliver presents to number 4, then number 7, then 9…' and so on.

Support
Ask the children to direct Father Christmas to houses following simple patterns rather than numbers, for example, to one side of the street, then the other, alternately.

Extension
Introduce odd and even numbers to the children and explain that odd-numbered houses are usually on one side of the road and even-numbered houses are on the other. Can the children label the houses in this manner?

Invite the children to play a game where they compete to deliver the parcels in the shortest amount of time, marking the house numbers with their own colour to show when a parcel has been delivered.

Home links
Ask parents and carers to walk in residential areas with their children and to point out house numbers and see which numbers their children recognize.

WINTER FESTIVAL

Christmas Day

Here, there and everywhere

Learning objective
To use everyday words to describe position.

Group size
Any size.

What you need
Card; collage materials, including gold shiny paper and cotton wool; backing paper; glue; scissors; Christmas tree (artificial, real or display); narrow ribbon in various colours; hole-punch; staple gun.

Preparation
Cover a wall with backing paper and stand the Christmas tree in front of the wall, perhaps stapling back branches to the wall to secure it.

What to do
Explain to the children that they are going to make Christmas-tree decorations to hang from the tree.

Discuss with the children the range of things they could create such as: a Christmas stocking – collaged with red shiny paper and edged with cotton wool; a Father Christmas – coloured or collaged; a snowman – outline of a snowman, covered with cotton wool, complete with black hat, pipe and buttons; a gold star – outline of a star covered with shiny gold paper, and so on. Let the children cut out and collage their decorations.

When the items are complete, punch a hole in the top of each of them and let the children choose the colour of ribbon to hang their decorations with. Encourage them to thread the ribbon themselves if they are confident, or do the threading for them, so that the decorations can be added to the tree.

Tell the children that you would like them to hang their decorations on the tree in turn. Provide instructions for each child, using positional language such as 'next to', 'beside', 'above', 'below', 'under' and so on.

Support
Offer plenty of supervision to the children in making their decorations, and use a more simple range of positional language in instructing them where to hang their decorations.

Extension
Once the tree is complete, encourage the children to describe the position of the different decorations using the appropriate vocabulary. Play a game seeing who can be first to spot a specified decoration and describe where it is to the rest of the group.

Invite the children to make a selection of presents to stand under the tree. These could be gifts wrapped in different-coloured papers or gifts of different sizes.

Home links
Ask parents and carers to use positional language when putting up Christmas decorations with their children at home. They could also reinforce positional language through daily tasks, such as putting away shopping.

Eid-ul-Fitr

Prayer patterns

What you need

Example of, or pictures of, a prayer mat; a selection of coloured paints; a range of plastic shapes for printing; protective table covering; aprons; A4 sheets of paper.

Preparation

Cover a table with a protective cloth and help the children to put on aprons. Put the paints in shallow dishes suitable for printing from. Draw an outline of a prayer mat for each child.

What to do

Explain to the children that Eid-ul-Fitr is a Muslim festival which marks the end of a month of fasting, known as Ramadan. During Ramadan, Muslims must attend the mosque to pray and carry out other religious duties. If possible, show the children either a real prayer mat or a picture of a prayer mat pointing out the size, shape, colour and patterns. Look closely at the pattern, picking out repeated lines and shapes.

Show the children the selection of plastic shapes and ask them to name each one and talk about its characteristics. Explain that you would like them to decorate their prayer mats using a selection of painted shapes.

Throughout this activity, reinforce the concept of recurring patterns by asking the children which shape will come next. Encourage them to describe the pattern to you saying which colour comes next, which shapes have been used and so on. Ask questions such as, 'Which colour/shape did you start with?', 'Which colour/shape will you finish with?' and so on.

When the prayer mats have been completed, display them with information about Ramadan.

Support

Ask the children to copy a pattern started by an adult that uses two simple shapes and two colours. As they become more confident, encourage them to follow more complex patterns.

Extension

Invite the children to create more complex patterns of their own.

Learning objective
To talk about, recognize and re-create simple patterns.

Group size
Any size.

Home links
Ask parents and carers to help their children to pick out patterns on carpets or mats and discuss whether they repeat, what colours they are and so on.

New gloves for the New Year

Learning objective
To use mathematical language in play.

Group size
Any size.

What you need
Selection of gloves and mittens in different shapes, sizes and colours; card; writing and drawing materials; pegs; baskets; play money; toy cash till; shopping bag; string; role-play furniture.

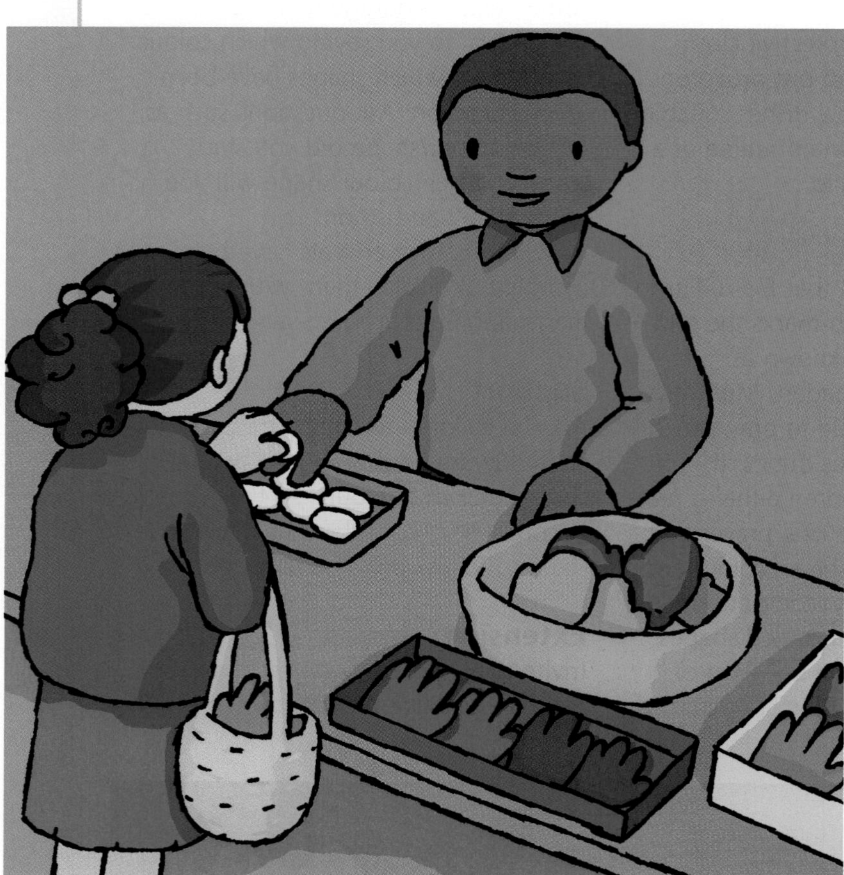

Preparation
Arrange the role-play furniture to represent a glove shop. Place the gloves and mittens in baskets, make pairs of mittens and gloves from card and peg them onto the washing line.

What to do
Explain to the children that at New Year people make resolutions about ways in which they would like to change. Ask the children if they know anyone who has made New Year's resolutions, or whether they have ever made any themselves, and whether or not they managed to keep them! What were these resolutions, and why did they make them?

Talk about how cold it is at the beginning of the year and explain that a good example of a New Year's resolution that the children could all make together could be to decide that they were always going to wrap up warm when it is cold.

Tell the children that to help them keep this resolution, the role-play area is now going to be a glove shop which will be used for number activities. These could include: matching, pairing and counting gloves; making shopping lists; buying gloves and giving change; arranging the items in patterns; sorting them in a variety of ways such as by colour.

Provide opportunities for the children to play in the glove shop with support from an adult if needed, and encourage the use of mathematical language at all times.

Support
Limit the activities available.

Extension
Provide simple work cards with instructions for the children to follow, such as, 'Hang two blue gloves on the line', 'Hang eight gloves on the line' and so on.

Home links
Ask parents and carers to help their children make a list of other things that come in pairs.

We three kings

Learning objective
To recognize and sort colours.

Group size
Groups of four children.

What you need

A copy of the photocopiable sheet on page 78 for each child; a dice numbered 1 to 3; selection of colouring materials.

Preparation

Number the shapes on the photocopiable sheet so that they can be coloured in by number.

What to do

Tell the children about the Epiphany. Explain that it celebrates the revelation to the Gentiles of Jesus Christ as the Saviour, as portrayed by the coming of the Three Wise Men.

Explain to the children that you would like them to play a game in which they will have to decorate the crowns of the Three Wise Men. Give each child in the group a photocopiable sheet and provide colouring materials and a dice for the children to share.

Before playing the game, reinforce the colour names and numbers using the key on the sheet. Discuss with the children their favourite colours and what they associate them with. To reinforce colour names, play simple games with the children, such as asking all the children with blue jumpers on to stand up, all the children with black shoes on to place their hands on their heads, and so on.

Now show the children how to play the game by throwing a dice and colouring in the corresponding numbered shape on the crown on the photocopiable sheet. Only one shape at a time may be coloured. The winner is the first to colour in all the shapes in the right colours.

Support

Adapt the photocopiable sheet by covering the numbers before photocopying it and using a dice marked with shapes rather than numbers.

Extension

Adapt the photocopiable sheet by changing the numbers to those of a greater value. The children could then play with two dice adding the numbers together to find out which shape to colour in.

Home links
Teach the children the song, 'We Three Kings' and invite parents and carers to practise it at home with their children.

Lucky money

Learning objectives
To use mathematical language in play; to begin to understand the concept of money.

Group size
Small groups.

What you need
Red paper; glue; number cards from 1 to 5; thick card; pencil; selection of coins; gold pens.

Preparation
Make envelopes with the red paper. Use the thick card to make a spinner, dividing it into five sections numbered 1 to 5.

What to do
Explain to the children that on Chinese New Year people get up early in the morning. Children are particularly happy at finding small red envelopes, filled with money and sweets, under their pillows.

Tell the children in your group that they are going to make 'lucky money' envelopes. Show them the selection of play money and go through the different values of the coins. Allow them to choose a number card, read the number and pick up that many coins for their envelope. Then ask each child to draw around the coins onto the front of their envelope, copying the value of each coin into its outline (1p, 2p, 5p and so on). Let the children decorate their envelopes with Chinese symbols using a gold pen.

When all the 'lucky money' envelopes have been completed, suggest to the children that they play a game to determine who will take home which envelope. Challenge the children to spin the spinner, in turn. Each child must choose the envelope with the amount of coins in corresponding to the number that the spinner lands on.

Support
Adapt the activity by inviting the children to complete rubbings of the coins onto the fronts of their envelopes, or by drawing the coin outlines for them, only asking them to write the values of the coins onto these. Do not play the game.

Extension
Ask each child to add together the total value of the coins in their envelope and to write this on the front of it.

To develop the children's knowledge further, play the game 'Guess the coin'. Choose a coin for the children to guess the value of and invite them to ask simple questions such as, 'Is it small?', 'Is it round?', 'Is it silver?' and so on.

Home links
Provide parents and carers with copies of the photocopiable sheet on page 79. Ask them to tell their children the year in which they were born and the animal this links to in the Chinese New Year.

Be my Valentine

What you need
Ready-made white fondant icing; food colouring; icing sugar; greaseproof paper; rolling pin; shape cutters; knives; stapler; doilies; aprons; protective table covering.

Preparation
Cover the table and ensure that all the children have washed their hands and are wearing aprons. Fold doilies in half, make them into a cone shape and secure with a staple. Make enough cones for each child to have one. Colour the fondant icing by kneading in a tiny drop of food colouring.

What to do
Explain that Valentine was a Christian Bishop of Rome who was imprisoned and fell in love with his gaoler's daughter, to whom he wrote a note signed, 'Your Valentine'. Explain to the children they are going to cut fondant icing into shapes for their loved ones.

Provide each child with a coloured ball of fondant icing. Talk about the shape and ask for ideas on other 3D shapes that it could be made into. Demonstrate making these different shapes, reinforcing some of their properties by telling the children, for example, 'A sphere will roll, it has one side', 'A cube has four corners and four sides, each side is the same length' and so on. Allow the children to cut or mould their own icing into a selection of different shapes.

Place the shapes on the greaseproof paper to dry and count them into the cones. Ask the children questions such as, 'How many shapes are in your cone?', 'What shapes do you have?', 'How many of each shape do you have?', 'Have you made any 3D shapes?' and so on.

Support
Limit the shapes to 'flat' 2D shapes, encouraging the children to use cutters.

Extension
Ask the children to record the number of different shapes in their cone.

Learning objective
To begin to use mathematical names for 'solid' 3D shapes and 'flat' 2D shapes and mathematical terms to describe shapes.

Group size
Small groups of four to six children.

Home links
Suggest that parents and carers make other shaped sweets at home with their child to bring and share.

Fill us up!

Learning objectives
To use language such as 'more' or 'less' to compare two numbers; to use mathematical language in everyday contexts.

Group size
Any size.

What you need

Equipment: sieve, bowl, wooden spoon, frying pan, spatula, plate, knife.
Ingredients: 4oz plain flour, 2 eggs, half pint milk, pinch of salt, 1 tablespoon oil.
Selection of fillings: jam, syrup, lemon, sugar.
Washing facilities; table covering; aprons; an enlarged copy of the photocopiable sheet on page 80; writing and drawing materials.

Preparation

Cover work-surface and ensure that all the children have washed their hands and are wearing aprons.

What to do

Explain that Shrove Tuesday is the day before Lent begins. Traditionally, on this day, Christians use up rich foods by making pancakes. Tell the children that they are going to prepare pancakes and make a record of what their favourite fillings are.

Begin by sieving the flour and salt into a bowl. Make a small hollow in the middle, add the eggs and half the milk and stir with a wooden spoon.

Gradually add the flour to the egg and milk while stirring. When the mixture is quite smooth, add the rest of the milk and stir. With the children at a safe distance, melt the oil in the pan until it is very hot (remember to emphasize safety when working with young children).

Pour in enough mixture to cover the bottom of the pan, cook and toss the pancake. When it is ready, turn it onto a plate, add a filling, roll and cut it into slices for the children to taste. Repeat this process several times until all the fillings have been used and all the children have had a taste.

To record the favourite filling, help the children to write their names on the enlarged photocopiable sheet. Ask questions such as, 'What is the most popular filling?', 'How many children like jam?', 'How many children like syrup more than sugar?', 'If one more person liked lemon, how many would there be?' and so on.

Support

Invite the children to discuss, in small groups or pairs, their preferences, likes and dislikes without having to record specific favourites.

Extension

Invite the children to collect their own data from a small group, filling in the names themselves on an individual photocopiable sheet.

Home links
Ask parents and carers to make pancakes at home, involving the children in the weighing process.

Rain or shine?

Throw and count

Colourful soldiers

Budding flowers

Pattern match

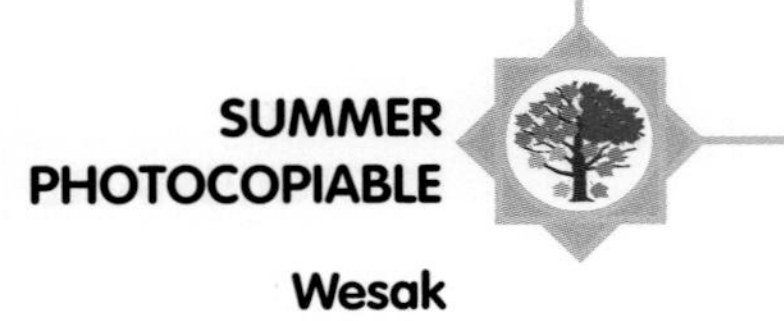

Which goes where?

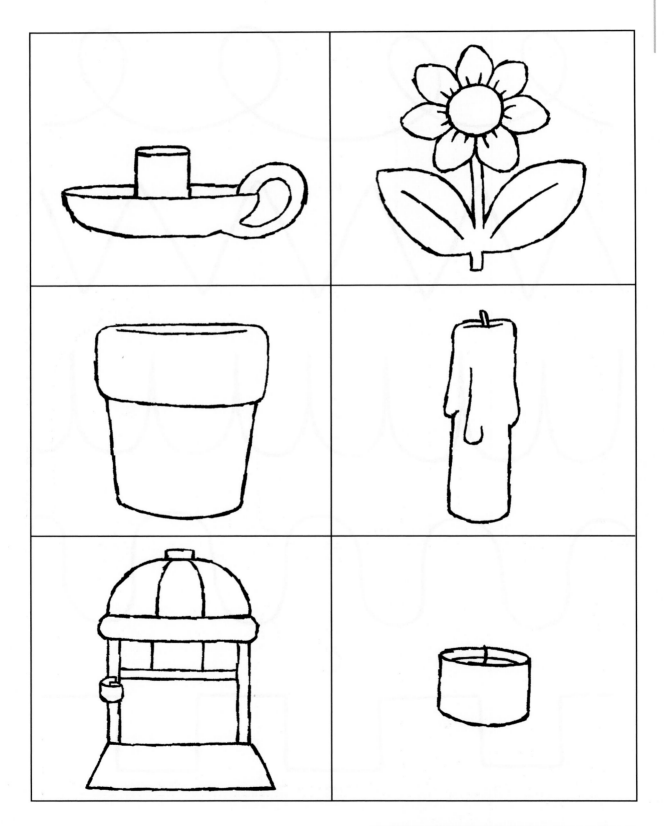

Pints of milk

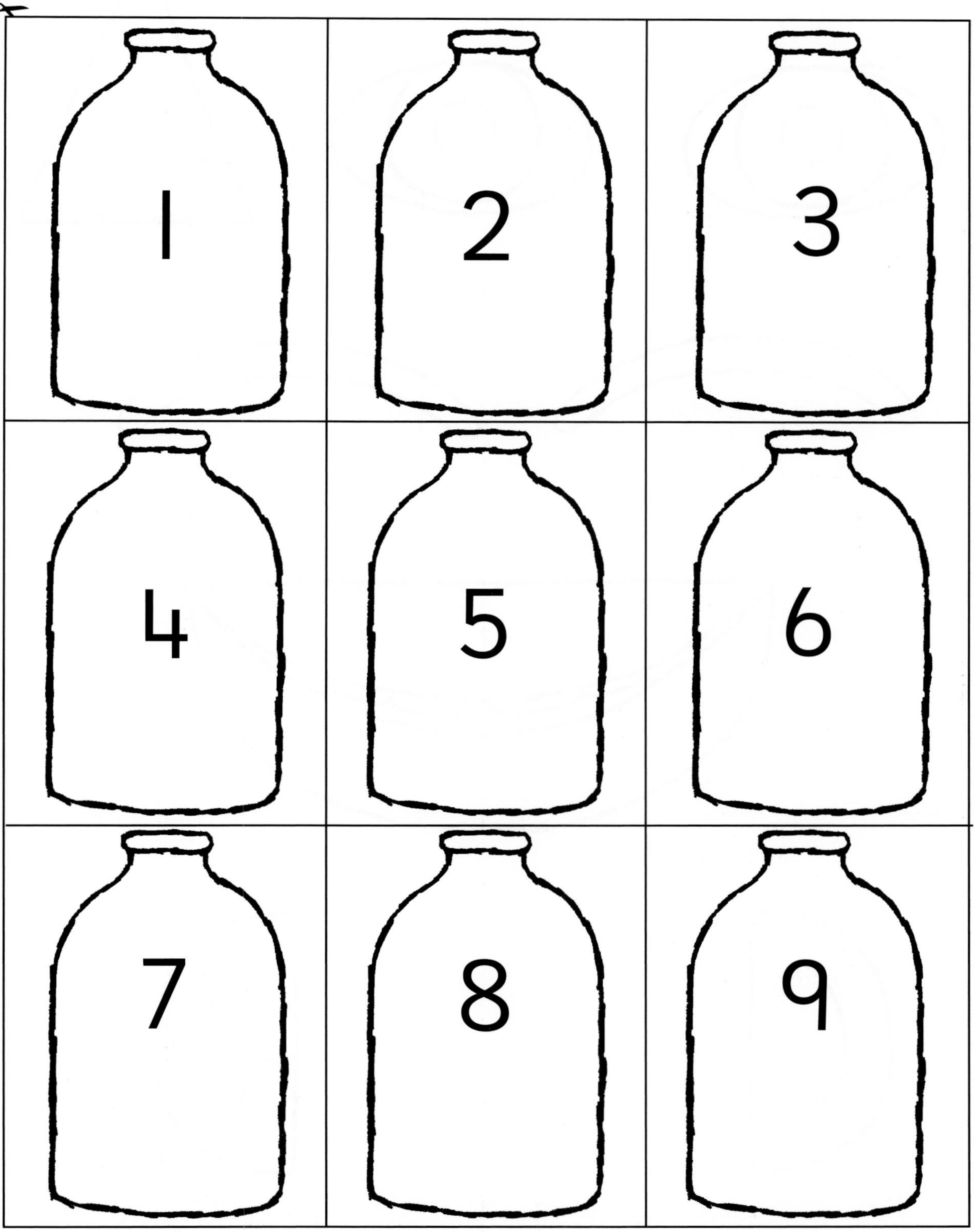

1	2	3
4	5	6
7	8	9

Shape up

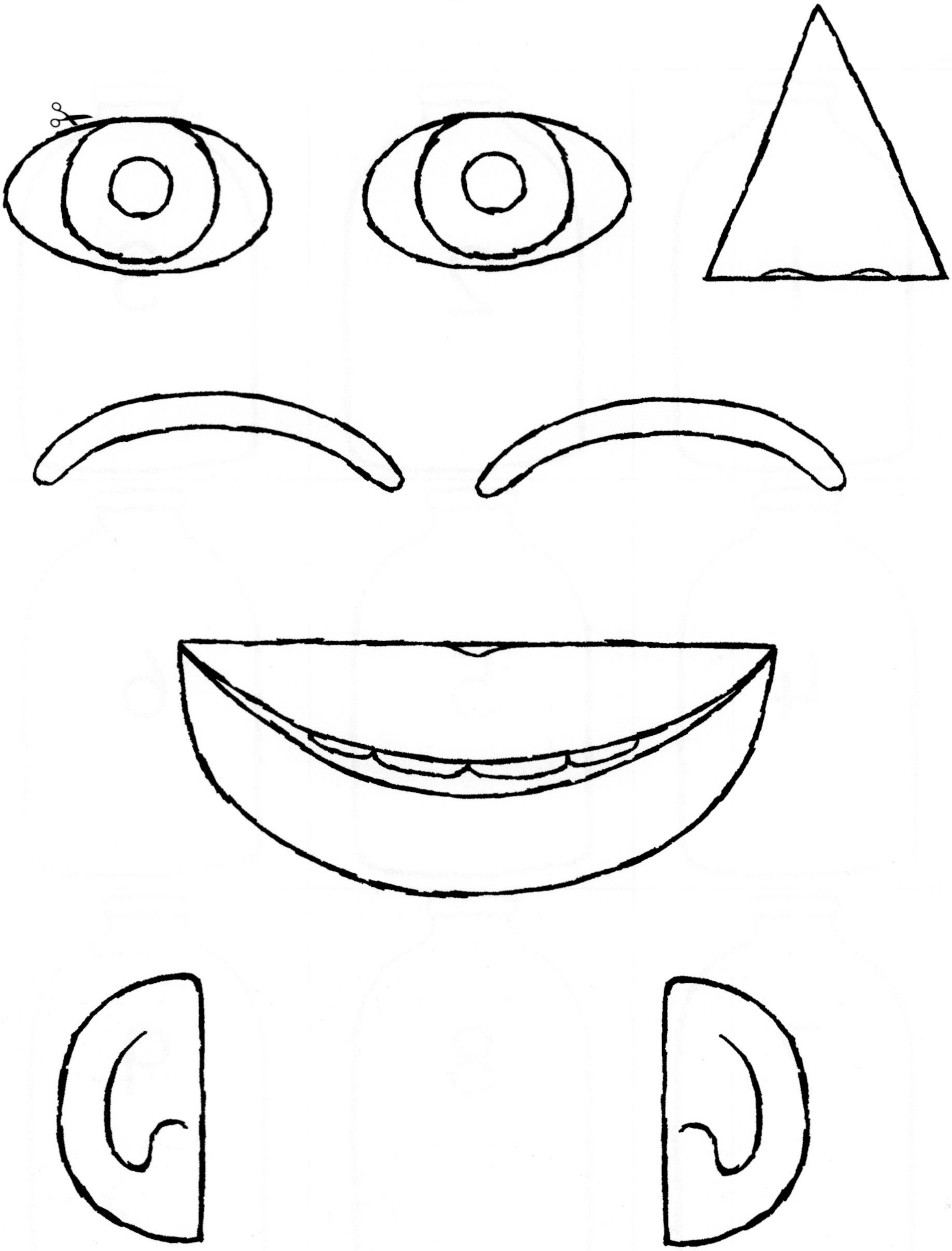

Fallen leaves

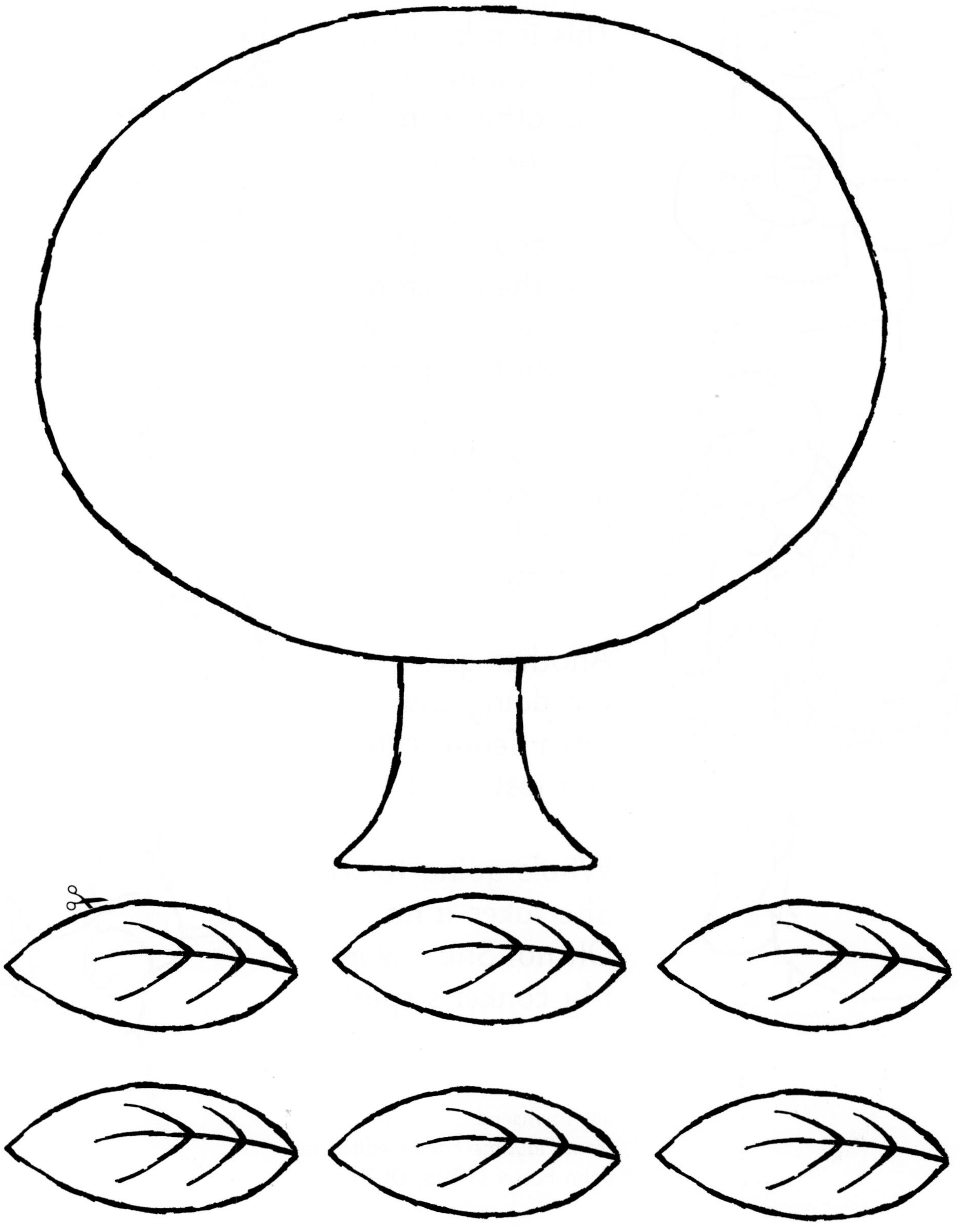

Conkers

This is a beauty,
brown and shiny.
The other conkers
all look tiny.

I thread the string
and then take aim.
I know I'm bound
to win the game.

I've had my go
and scored a hit.
Now Jenny tries
and misses it.

Another go
I'm doing well.
Then Jenny's turn.
You just can't tell

Who's going to win.
She takes a hit
Oh no! She's won!
My conker's split!

Jill Townsend
from *Playtime Poems* edited by
John Foster (1995, OUP)

Whose hand is it?

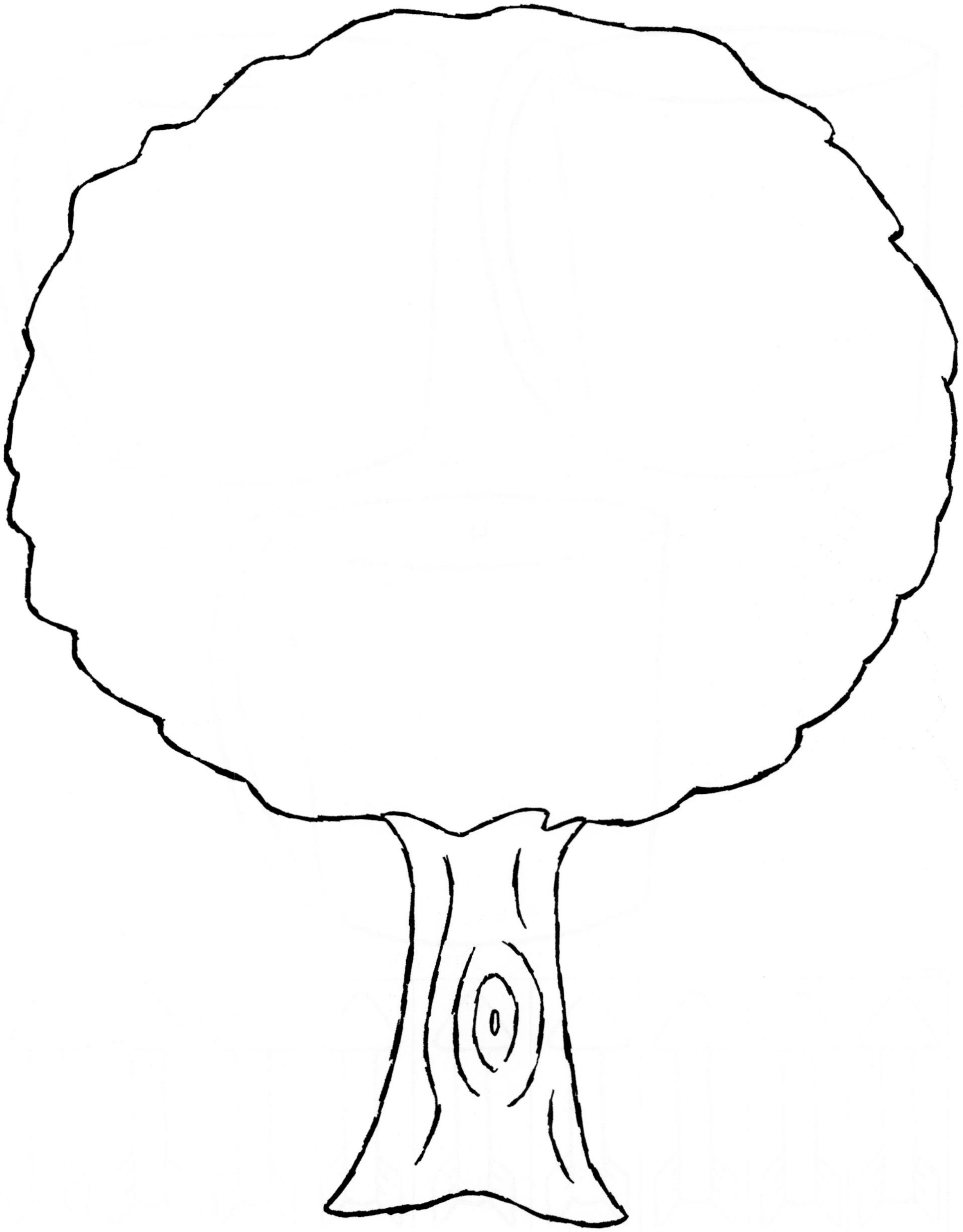

Aim, fire!

3

2

4

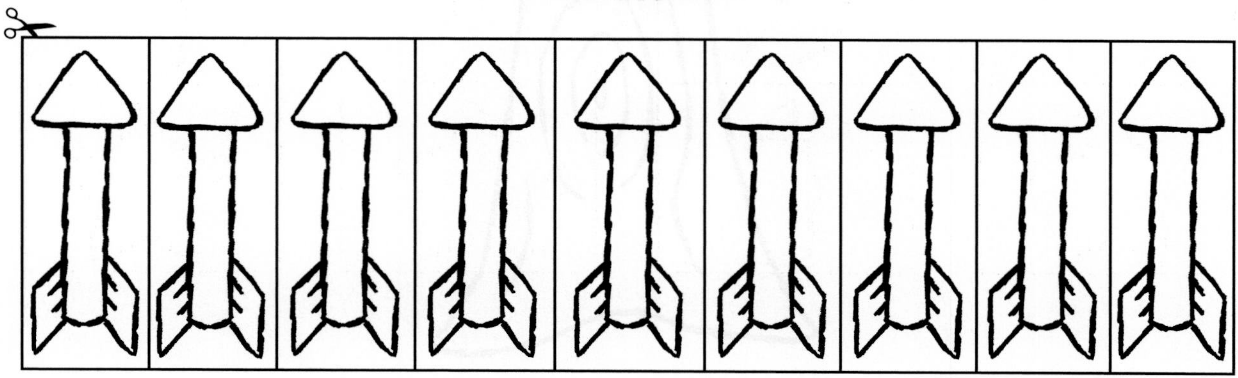

Light it up

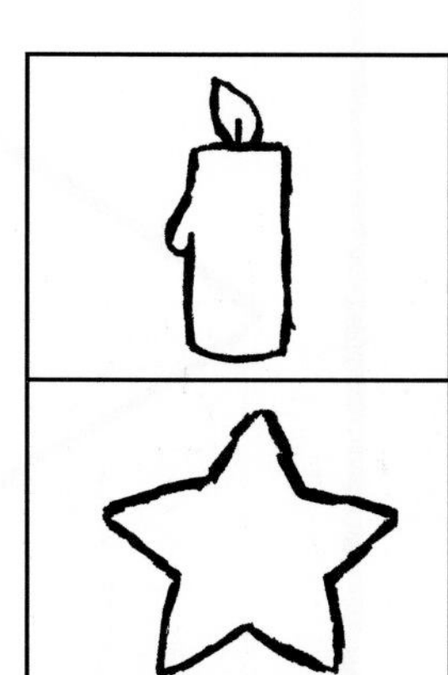

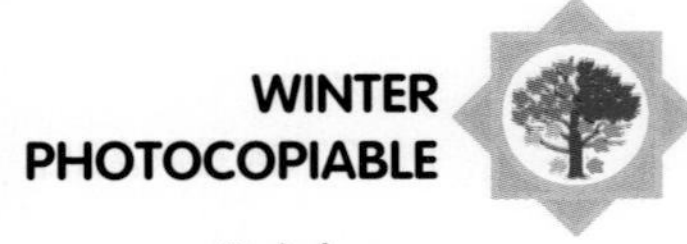

We three kings

1 2 3

1 2 3

1 2 3

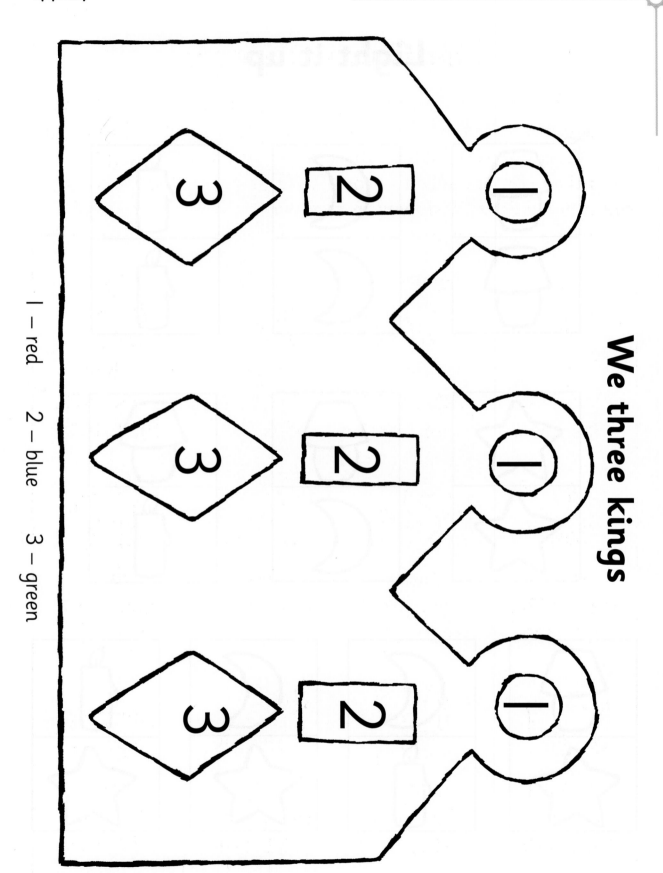

1 – red 2 – blue 3 – green

The Chinese years

Legend has it that 12 animals were chosen by Chinese Gods to represent the years. The animals argued about who should be first. The Gods resolved the matter by having a race across a big river. Rat travelled on ox's back, just winning the race. The other animals followed in sequence.

rat 1960, 1972, 1984, 1996	ox 1961, 1973, 1985, 1997	tiger 1962, 1974, 1986, 1998	rabbit 1963, 1975, 1987, 1999

dragon 1964, 1976, 1988, 2000	snake 1965, 1977, 1989, 2001	horse 1954, 1966, 1978, 1990	ram 1955, 1967, 1979, 1991

monkey 1956, 1968, 1980, 1992	cockerel 1957, 1969, 1981, 1993	dog 1958, 1970, 1982, 1994	pig 1959, 1971, 1983, 1995

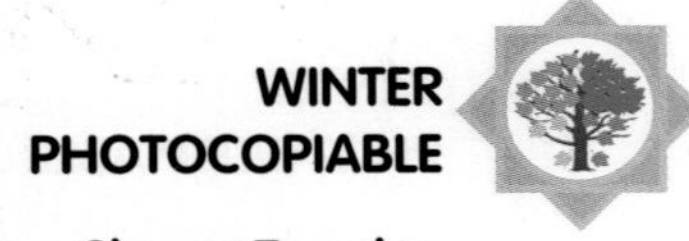

Fill us up!

jam

syrup

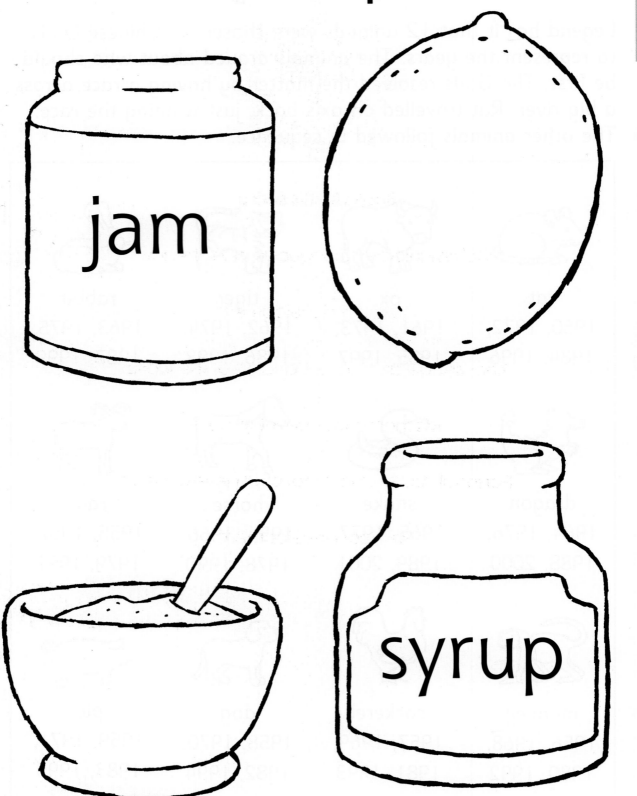